Caspar David Friedrich
A–Z

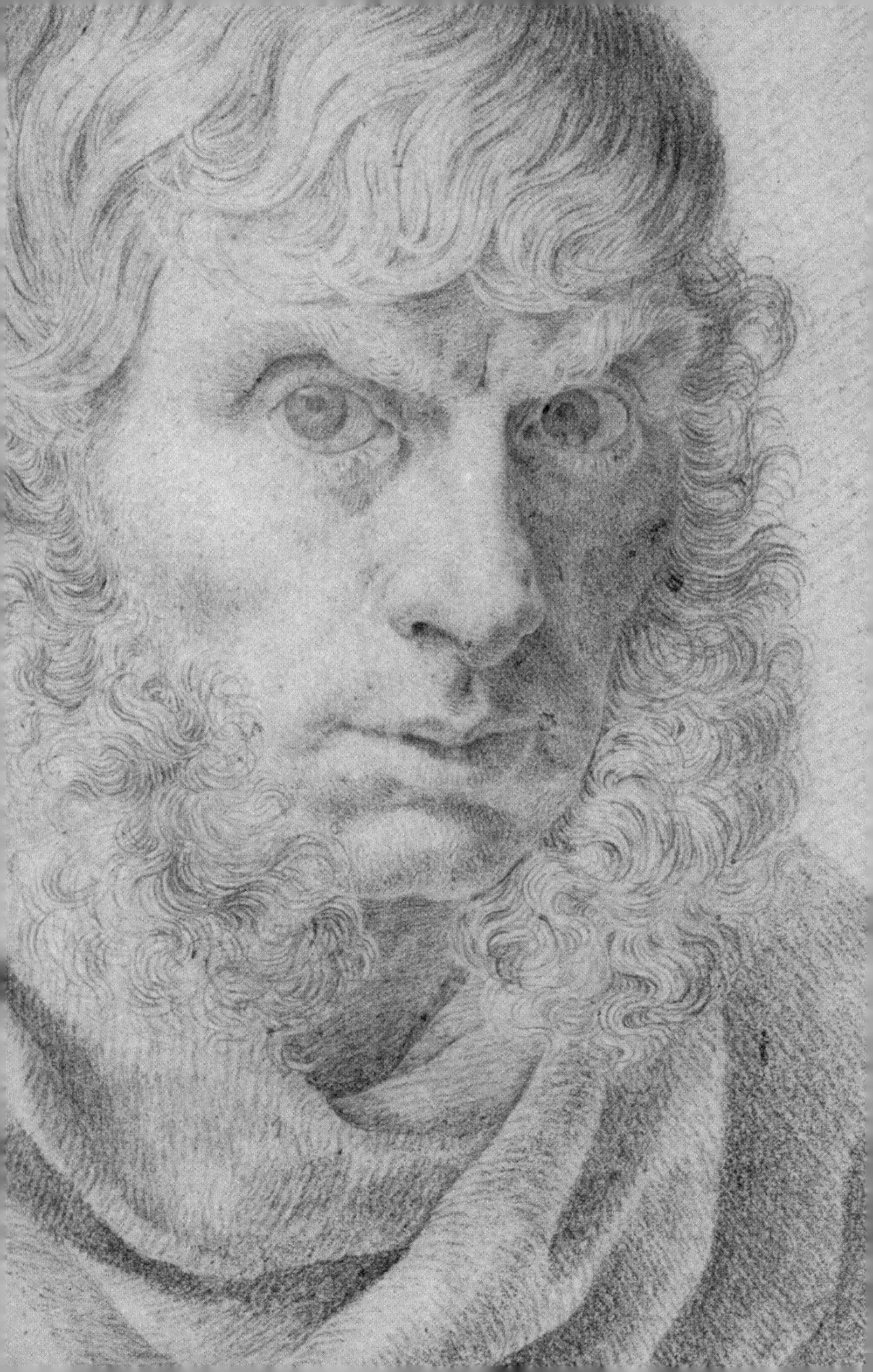

Caspar David Friedrich
A–Z

Barbara Hess

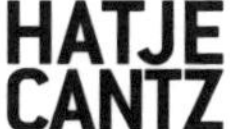

A→ A Solitary Tree
B→ Bride
C→ Chasseur
D→ Dresden
E→ Eternity
F→ Fog
G→ Greifswald
H→ Harbor
I→ Inwardness
J→ Jeers
K→ Kersting
L→ Last Generation
M→ Moon
N→ Northwest Passage
O→ Owl
P→ Politics
Q→ Quistorp
R→ Rearview Figure
S→ Sepia
T→ Transparent
U→ Under Construction
V→ View
W→ Wanderer
X→ Xylography
Y→ Young's *Night-Thoughts*
Z→ Zittau Mountains

A → A Solitary Tree

In her writings, the American philosopher Donna Haraway appeals to us to "make kin," that is, to make ourselves related with other lifeforms beyond the confines of our own species. This could lead to relationships across species that are not based on exploitation and destruction. Perhaps Friedrich already had such relationships in mind. In any case, a letter of the Russian poet Vasily Zhukovsky from June 1821 seems to suggest this. He reports that Friedrich's "favorite subject" in conversations was nature, "which he treated like a family member."[1]

In Friedrich's *Village Landscape in the Morning Light (Solitary Tree)* from 1822, the focus of the composition is on a monumental oak tree. The two usual working titles do not originate from the artist himself, but rather from a later period. It thus remains open whether this is in fact the representation of a morning mood. The central tree also need not be perceived as "solitary"; several congeners stand to the left and right of it, and the tiny figure of the shepherd leaning against the trunk appears to nearly merge with the tree.

Friedrich's contemporaries would often have read the painting with national and religious aspects in mind. For the Protestant pastor and poet Ludwig Gotthard Kosegarten, who Friedrich knew through his drawing teacher Quistorp,→Quistorp the oak was the "Tree of God" due to its permanence.[2] The oak has also been a German national symbol for centuries, which is today found, for example, in the motif of the oak branch on the copper-clad German euro cent coins. Oak leaves also play a role in many, not only German, crests and military honors. Most conspicuous about Friedrich's composition is how subordinated those pictorial elements are that refer to human existence. The roofs of the houses in the village settlement, with their trails of smoke and the church spires that protrude over the border of the green valley, are literally marginal manifestations in the landscape.

Village Landscape in the Morning Light (Solitary Tree) 1822
Oil on canvas 55 × 71 cm
Alte Nationalgalerie, Staatliche Museen zu Berlin

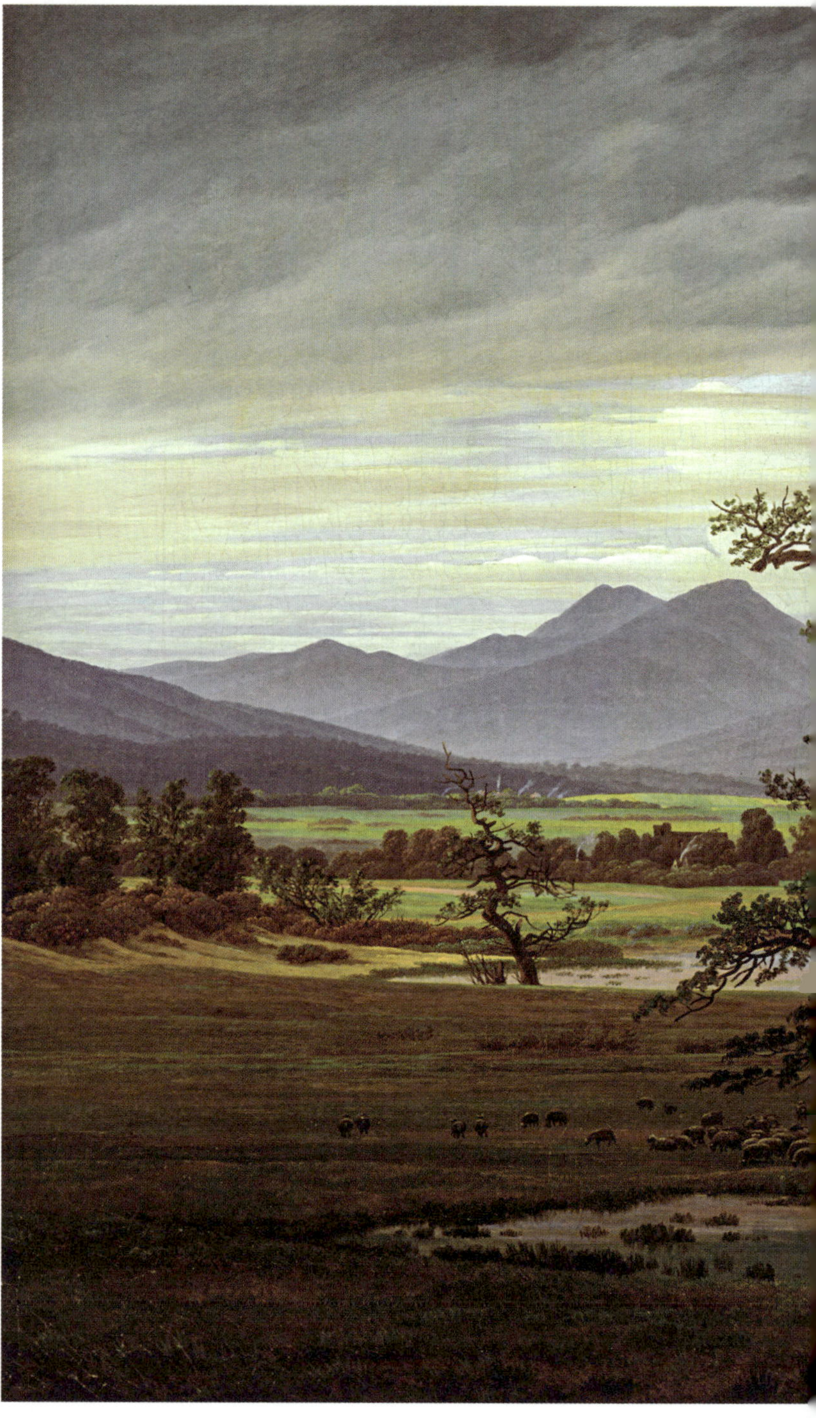

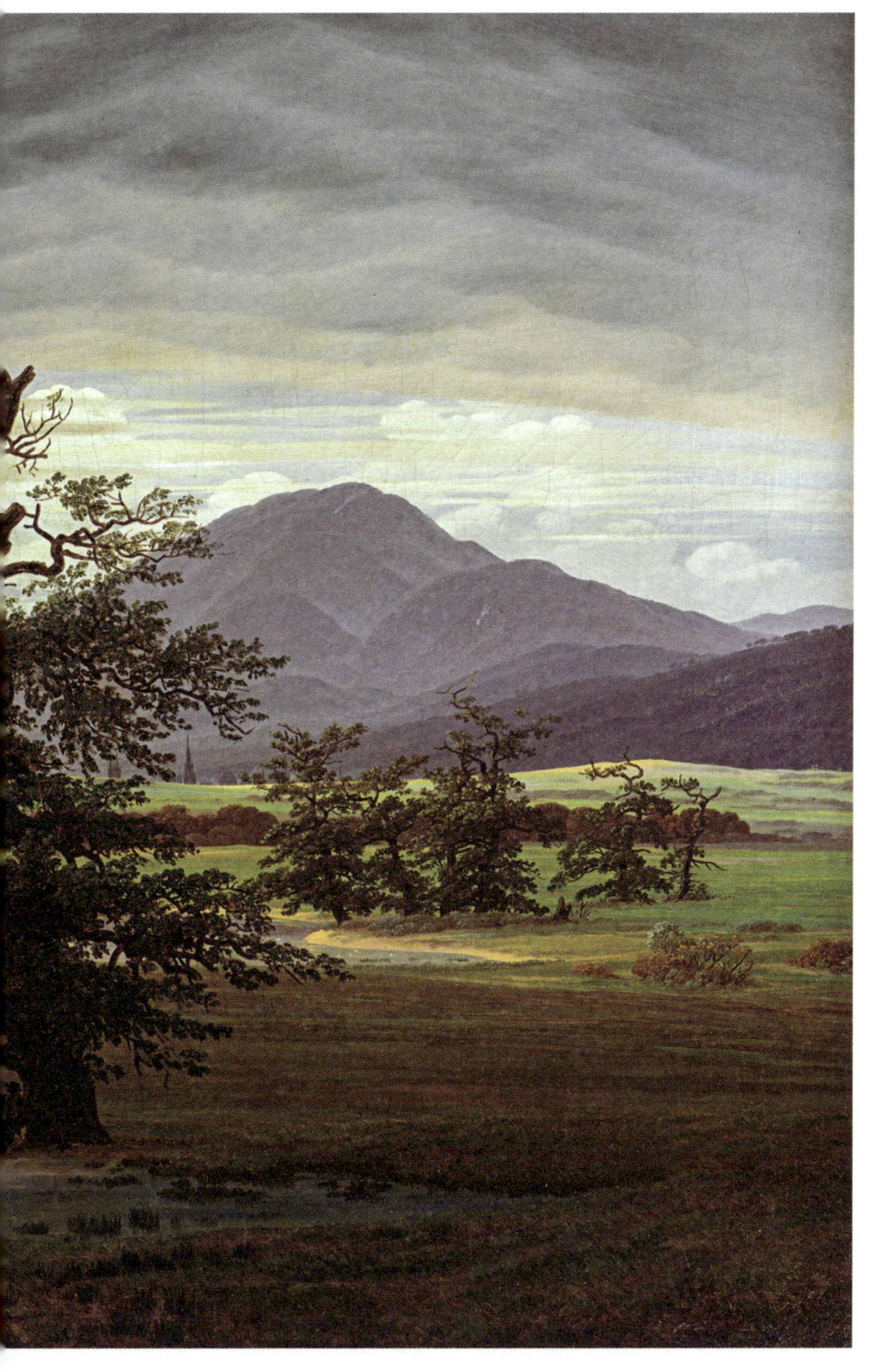

B → Bride

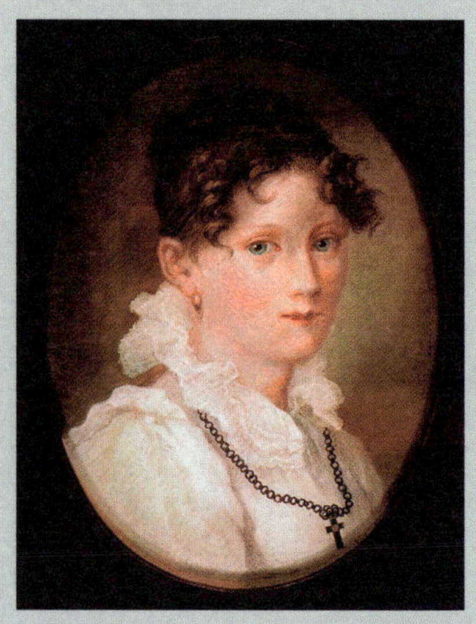

It appears to have surprised the artist's circle of friends when Caspar David Friedrich and Caroline Bommer exchanged vows in January 1818 in Dresden.→Dresden Helene von Kügelgen, who, together with her husband, Gerhard von Kügelgen, were among Friedrich's confidantes, referred to him as "the most un-couplish of all un-couplish people." Several of the most familiar paintings of Friedrich—such as *Chalk Cliffs on Rügen* →p. 13 and *Woman before the Setting* (or: *Rising*) *Sun* →p. 83—are linked with this reversal. In the summer of 1818, the couple traveled to Greifswald to Friedrich's family and to Rügen, where Friedrich had already previously drawn during his hikes and had gathered motifs like Cape Arkona →p. 86 for his compositions.

Chalk Cliffs on Rügen is often seen as a wedding painting but presents puzzles. This is because it doesn't show, as might be expected, a couple, but rather three figures that have arrived at a precipice. The woman is holding onto tree roots and points into the depths, while a male figure in old German costume at the right edge of the painting defies the dizzying situation and gazes assuredly out to sea, where two small boats are sailing—most likely symbols of the journey of life. A second male figure is lying on the ground in the middle. He has put aside his hat and staff and gropes his way to the edge of the steep coast on his belly—as if he feared falling. At the top edge of the painting, the branches of two trees interlock as if in an embrace and form a heart shape in the foreground with the tree trunks and the grassy plateau. The scenery is not a topographically precise reproduction of the famous chalk cliffs on Rügen, but is instead composed by Friedrich, just as the two trees are his addition.

Friedrich did not date and title his oil paintings, which expands space for interpretation. The *Woman before the Setting* (or: *Rising*) *Sun* is a good example of this.[3] The painting, approximately as large as a DIN A4 sheet of paper, is usually dated with 1818 and seen as a painting of Friedrich's wife, who might have been pregnant with the couple's first child at this time; the woman represented welcomes the coming day, which could also stand metaphorically for new life, with a gesture of reverence or adoration. However, the back-figure remains anonymous and thus a projection surface that invites further interpretations—for example, the painting was already produced several years prior to the wedding and the woman represented is an early love of Friedrich, Juliane Stoye.[4] What is unmistakable, however, is that Friedrich did not designate the central female figure either as wife or expecting mother, but instead focuses exclusively on a landscape experience as such.

Traugott Pochmann
Portrait of Caroline Friedrich **ca. 1824**
Oil on canvas
Private Collection

Chalk Cliffs on Rügen **1818**
Oil on canvas 90.8 × 70.6 cm
Kunst Museum Winterthur/
Reinhart am Stadtgarten

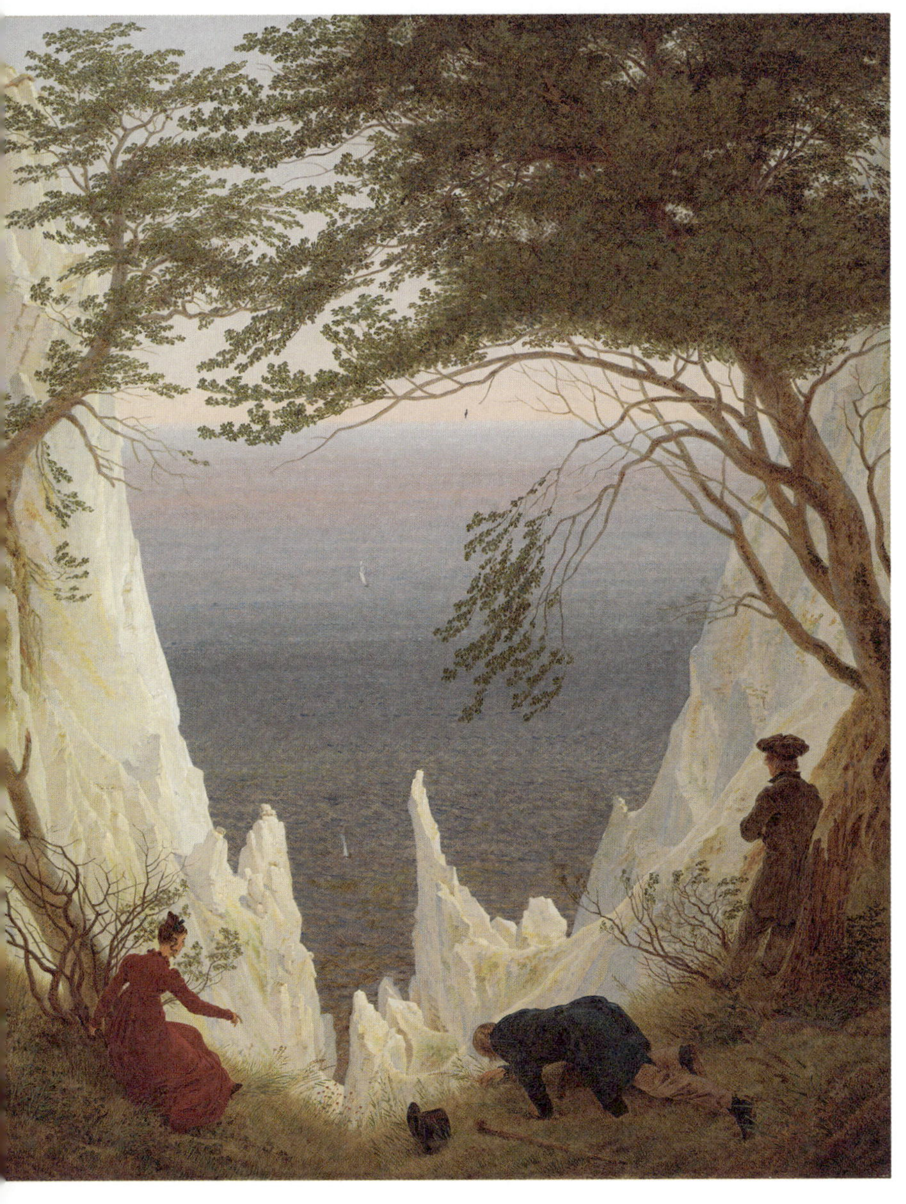

c → Chasseur

The description that Heinrich von Kleist had found for *Monk by the Sea* suits *Chasseur in the Forest*: he is "the lonely center point in the lonely circle." → Young's *Night-Thoughts* At the same time, he is a lonely exception among the many "back-figures," the figures with their backs turned to the viewer, for which Friedrich is famous. This is because the *Chasseur* is literally an image of the enemy. His uniform identifies him as a French soldier. The French troops had conquered and occupied large parts of Europe in the Napoleonic Wars since 1800, including Friedrich's home region of Swedish Pomerania. They had been decisively defeated at the Battle of Leipzig in October 1813. Friedrich himself did not fight in the wars of liberation from 1813 to 1815, but participated financially in the outfitting of his friend Georg Friedrich Kersting.[5] → Kersting

The *Chasseur* appears to be fighting a losing battle, as if surrounded by a gloomy fir forest. Behind him is a fork in the road with two tree trunks; a raven is perched on one as a symbol of death, singing him "a song of death," as a contemporary reviewer opined.[6] He becomes an imaginary target, depicted from an elevated, unspecified standpoint. Friedrich made no secret of his anti-French sentiments. He wrote to his brother Christian, who was staying in Lyon in November 1808: "You can feel yourself that it is not right for you to be in France as a German, and that still comforts me somewhat, because I would otherwise entirely doubt your

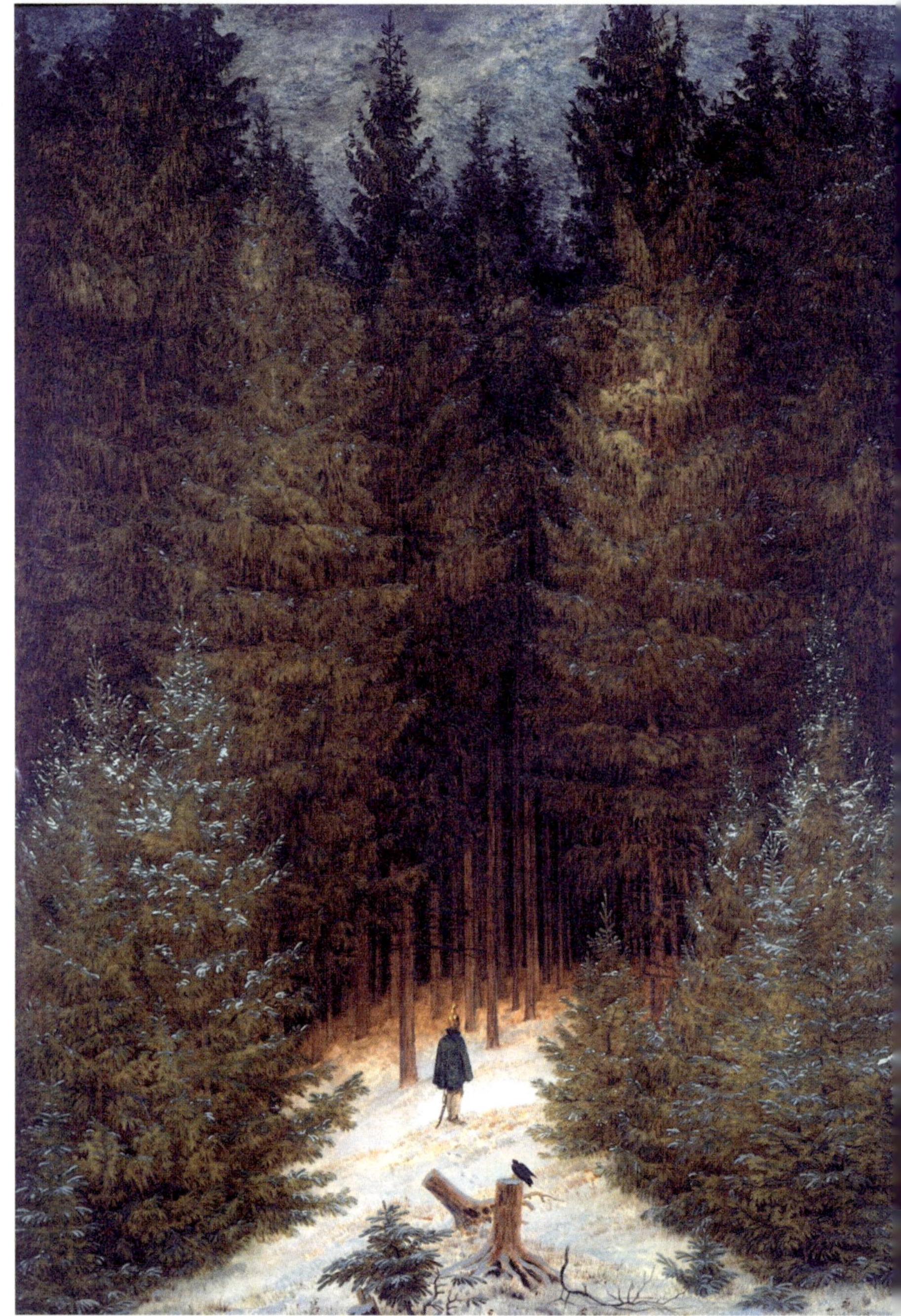

Germanness."[7] Despite Friedrich's clear aversion to the military opponent, the sight of the *Chasseur* rouses ambivalent emotions. The painting conveys the impression that the fate of the soldier is sealed but does not appeal to feelings of triumph. This is because the back-figure always invites viewers to put themselves in its place.

Chasseur in the Forest **ca. 1813**
Oil on canvas 65.7 × 46.7 cm
Private Collection

D → Dresden

Friedrich settled in Dresden in the autumn of 1798 to continue his art studies, which he had begun in Copenhagen, at the academy there. Several reasons spoke in favor of this, including the "proximity of the most splendid art treasures";[8] the Saxon Elector August the Strong (1670–1733) and his son August III (1696–1763) had compiled important collections and had buildings erected that prompted epithets for the city at the beginning of the nineteenth century like "German Florence" or "Florence on the Elbe." Friedrich also praised that Dresden was "surrounded by beautiful nature." The landscape painters Adrian Zingg (1734–1816) and Johann Christian Klengel (1751–1824) also taught at the academy, from whom Friedrich may have hoped for impulses for his future development.[9]

Friedrich lived in the Saxon royal capital until the end of his life in 1840 with brief interruptions. However, his hope of becoming Klengel's successor at the academy and to thus also secure his material existence was disappointed in the mid-1820s. There was no artistic or political consensus with regard to Friedrich at this time. Many found his painting to be too mystical and dark, too individualistic. In political terms, he obviously opposed the restoration of the old feudal order following the Vienna Congress of 1814–15, which was also known to the Saxon authorities.[10]

Friedrich doubtlessly justified his reputation as an individualist with *The Large Enclosure near*

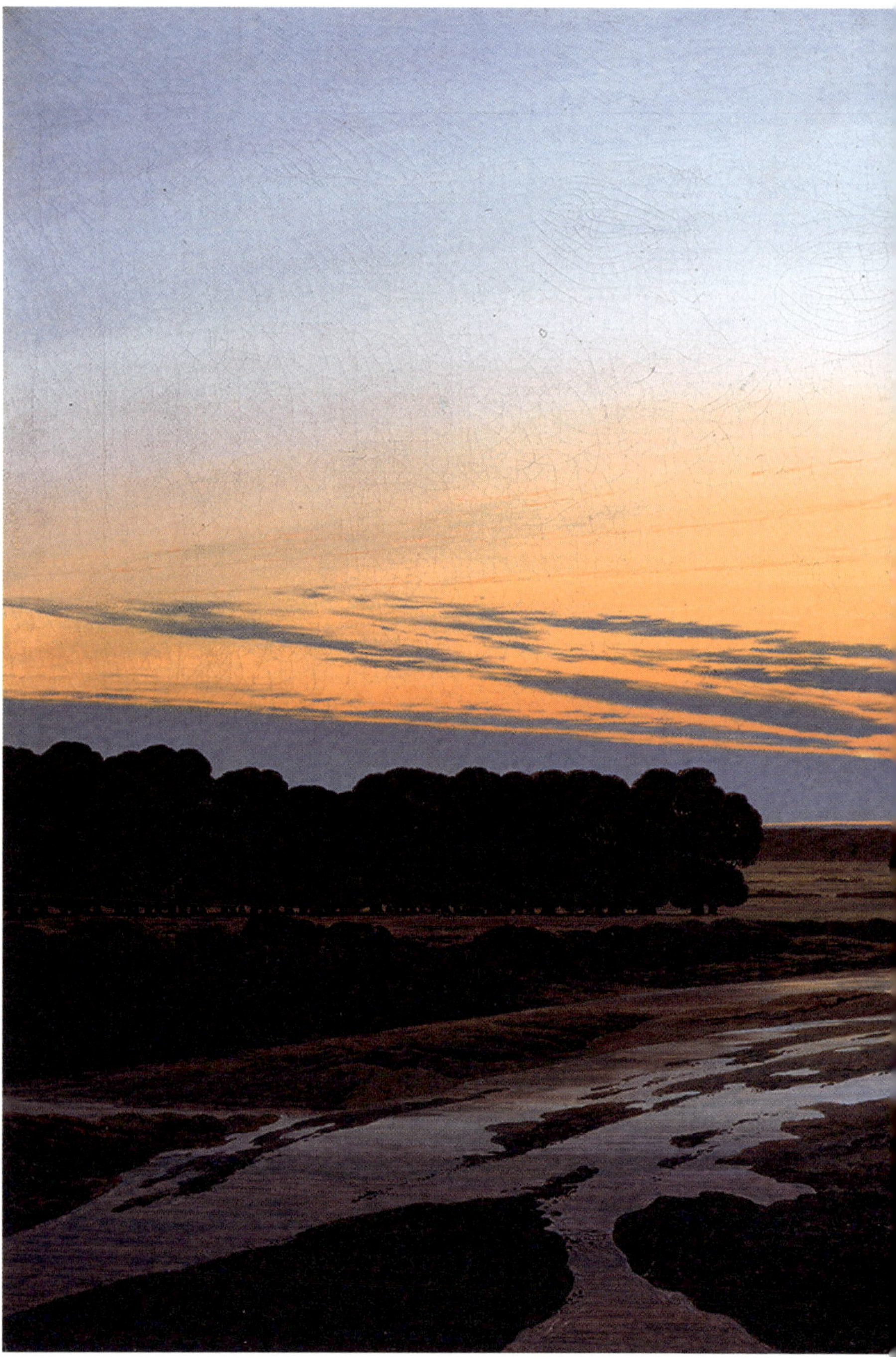

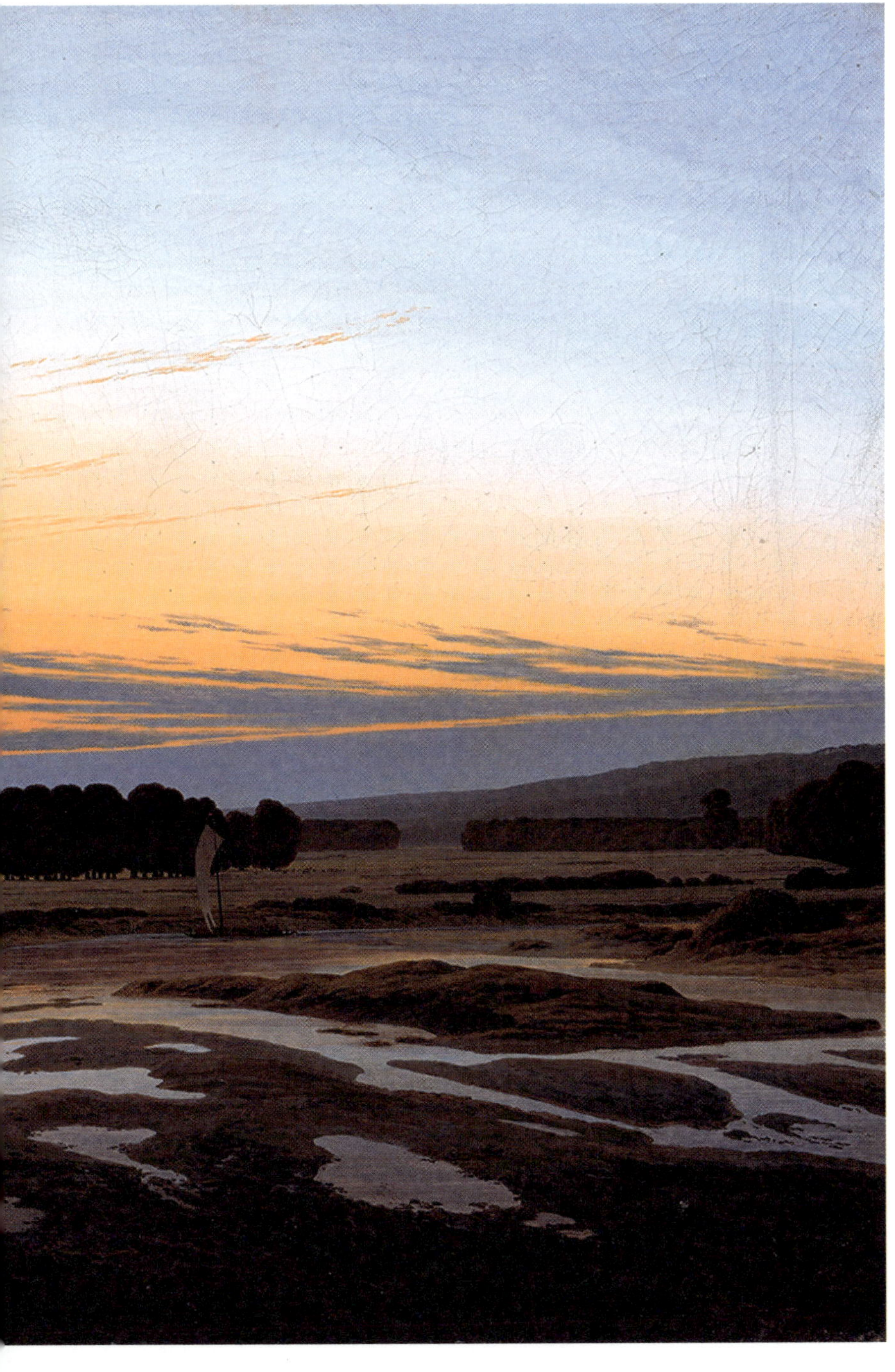

Dresden (around 1832). There is also no comparable work in his own oeuvre. The title refers to the Große Ostragehege, a pasture landscape in the northwestern area of Dresden. However, the painting shows a scene like it is from another planet. It breaks with conventions of representation and seeing in a dual respect. The point of view from which the unreal scene is seen appears to float over the landscape. The foreground with the insular sandbanks and the sky are not represented according to the rules of central perspective, but instead appear arched. They describe a hyperbola, thus an endless curve of two separate branches that are symmetrical with one another—a construction with which Friedrich had worked often.→ Under Construction The impression thus arises of a mysterious correspondence between heaven and earth, which is reinforced by the reflection of the sky in the water.

***The Large Enclosure near Dresden* ca. 1832**
Oil on canvas 73.5 × 102.5 cm
Galerie Neue Meister, Staatliche Kunstsammlungen Dresden

E → Eternity

By around 1820, Friedrich's art appeared to come from a different era. "Year after year Friedrich stumbles ever deeper into the thick fog →Fog of mysticism. Nothing is foggy or weird enough for him," one critic found. "His pictures have already in part stopped being works of art."[11] The withering judgment indicates how willful Friedrich's pictorial inventions seemed at that time.

Toward the end of his life, the artist himself trusted that time was on his side. "I have no intention of working against the dictates of the day, of swimming against the current, when such dictates are purely a matter of fashion," he wrote in around 1830. "But much less am I so weak as to do obeisance to the demands of the age when they go against my convictions. I spin about me my chrysalis, and let others do the same; and I leave it to time to decide what shall come of it, whether a brilliant butterfly →p. 107 or a maggot."[12] Friedrich's place today as a central figure of Romanticism and the great public interest in his art likely exceed all his expectations.

Friedrich dedicated several cohesive work groups to the passing of time. His cycles of times of day and seasons at the same time stand for the stages of life. He finds images for becoming and passing, which are in no sense "foggy," but are instead rather explicit, as in the case of the two skeletons in a limestone cave and

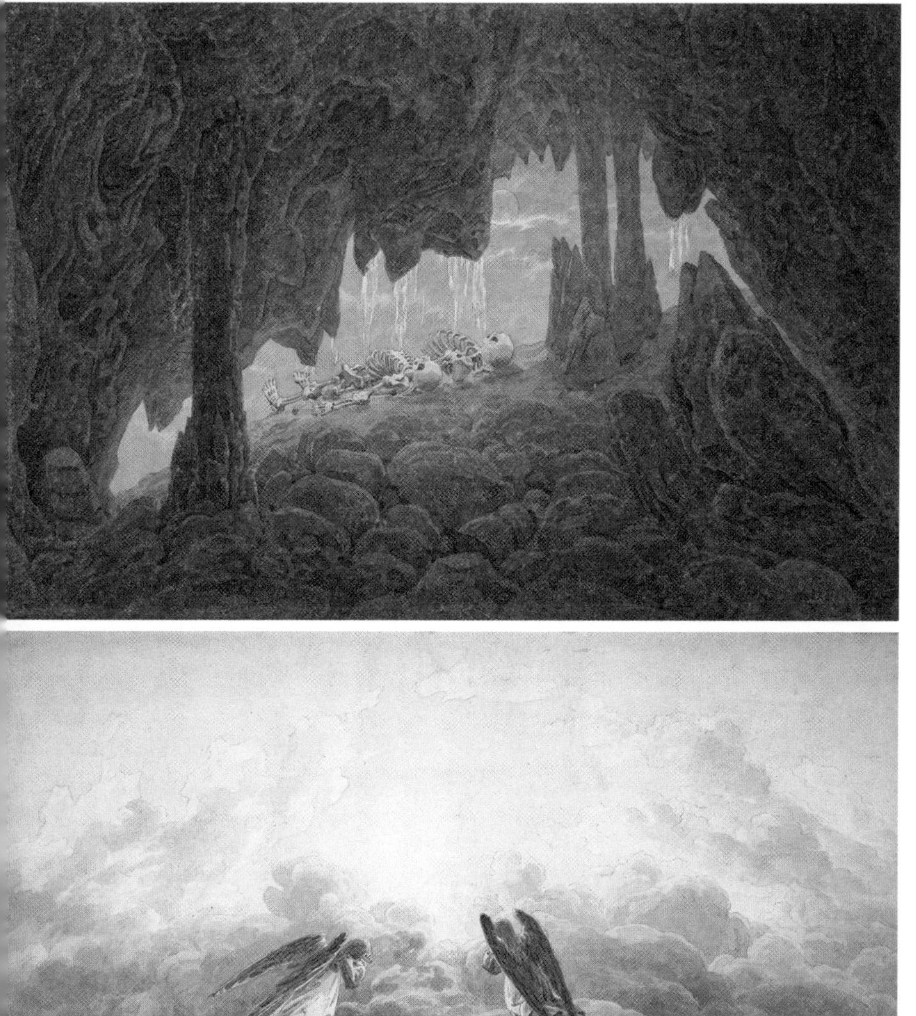

the two adoring angels floating above the clouds.→p. 25 In his imagination, he had the privilege of seeing beyond the edges of his own lifetime and era.

Skeletons in a Cave with Stalactites **ca. 1826**
From the Stages of Life series
Pencil on velin with brown wash 18.8 × 27.5 cm
Hamburger Kunsthalle, Kupferstichkabinett

Angels in Adoration **ca. 1826**
From the Stages of Life series
Pencil on velin with brown wash 18.5 × 26.7 cm
Hamburger Kunsthalle, Kupferstichkabinett

F → Fog

Friedrich embarked on new terrain in around 1807 with the *Sea Beach in the Fog* oil painting. Up to this point, he had drawn and worked with watercolor and gouache and made a name for himself with large-format sepias.→Sepia In *Sea Beach in the Fog,* he transferred the tonal transitions of the sepia technique, which generate atmospheric light effects, to painting. The medium itself—its possibility to show or conceal something—also becomes the theme here. A narrow shore zone can be seen in the foreground of the painting; an anchor and two forked, crutch-like sticks that fishermen set up to hang their nets on lie there. One can not only see these things as everyday work instruments, but also ascribe symbolic meaning to them. Thus, the anchor could stand for hope and the rowing boat for a bark that transports the dead into the realm beyond.[13]

An approximately equal sized counterpart was produced in the same year. *Sea Beach with Fisherman* shows a similar landscape, but conveys a contrasting mood. The shore area is covered with grass and shrubs, the weirs are hanging in an orderly fashion, and a fisherman gazes at the peaceful water on a low rise in the middle of the strip of shore. The sky is brightening over the deep horizon. Friedrich himself described what the changes to the landscape that motivate the pair of paintings could elicit in him: "Today, for the first time, the otherwise so beautiful area calls out to me transience and death, as it usually only smiled at me with joy and life," he noted in his journal in 1803. "All of nature lies faded before me."[14]

Sea Beach in the Fog is not only an image of disorientation and the intangible. With its indefiniteness, it also offers space for subjectivity and perhaps even visualizes the cottony soft feeling in the head known today as brain fog.

Seashore in the Fog 1807
Oil on canvas 34.2 × 50.2 cm
Österreichische Galerie Belvedere, Vienna

Seashore with Fisherman 1807
Oil on canvas 33.5 × 51 cm
Österreichische Galerie Belvedere, Vienna

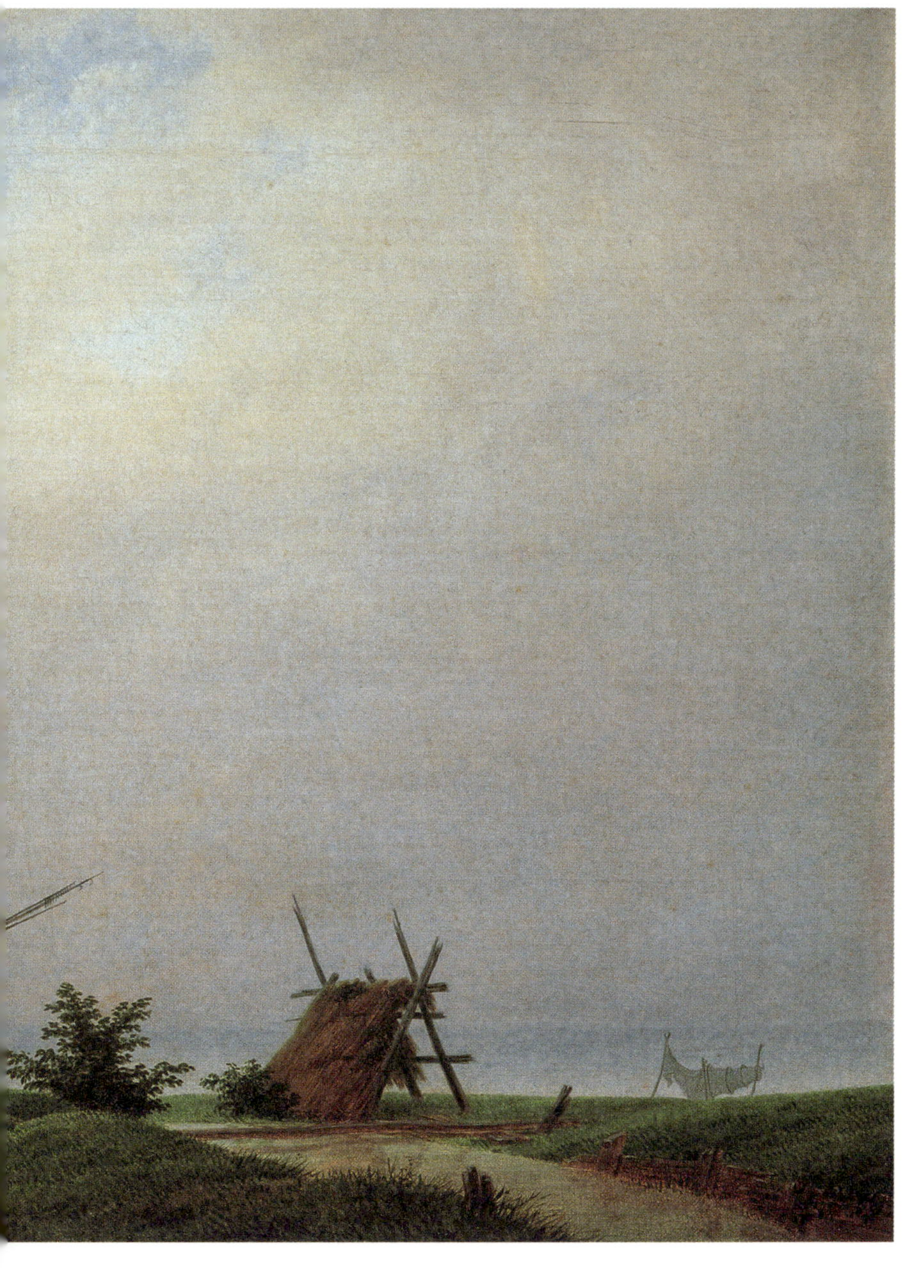

G → Greifswald

Caspar David Friedrich was born on September 5, 1774, in Greifswald. The city had been Lutheran since 1538, and Friedrich's family home—like Friedrich's later understanding of art—was also defined by the Protestant faith. His father, Adolf Gottlieb Friedrich (1730–1809), had already acquired the residence in the Lange Straße, where the Caspar David Friedrich Centre is found today, in the 1760s. He operated workshops there as a "fabricant and wholesale merchant in soap and light"—*Licht* (light) was a word for candles at that time. The artist lost his mother, Sophie Dorothea née Bechly (1747–1781) early on. She left behind a husband and ten children, who were cared for by a housekeeper after her death.

The old Hanseatic and university city, which had belonged to the Kingdom of Sweden since the Peace of Westphalia of 1648 and had hardly five thousand inhabitants at the time of Friedrich's birth lies in Western Pomerania on the southern Baltic Sea, where the River Ryck flows into a lagoon, the Bay of Greifswald. Even though Friedrich settled permanently in Dresden in 1798 after studying in Copenhagen, he returned to his hometown regularly and found many familiar motifs of his work—the Greifswald port with its sailing vessels, the monastery ruins in the Eldena district or the island of Rügen off the coast with its famous chalk cliffs—there and in the immediate vicinity.

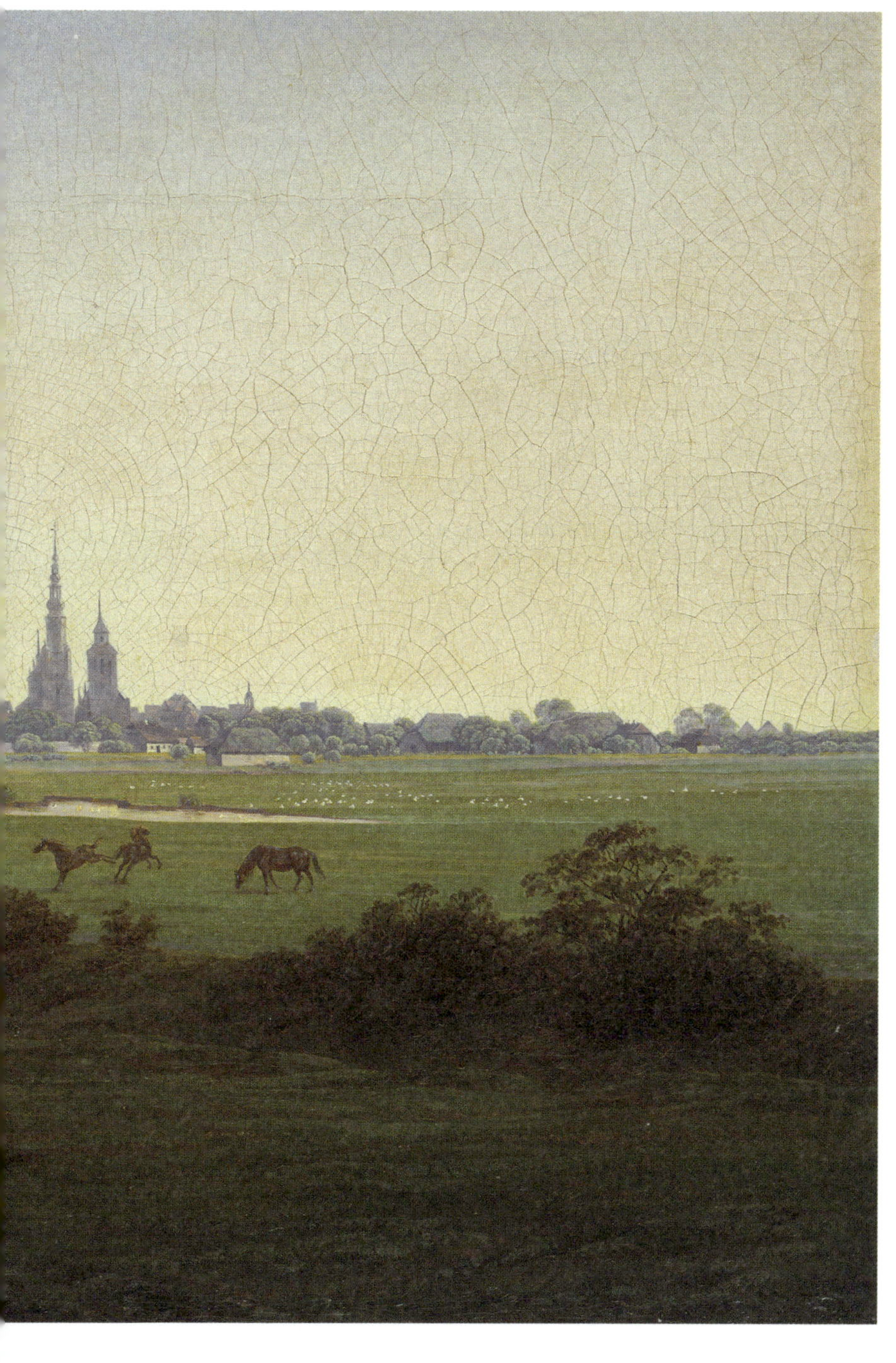

Meadow near Greifswald → pp. 36–37 seems to have originated at the beginning of the 1820s and shows the city from the west from a distance, which is emphasized by the dark zone in the foreground marked by a wall of earth and shrubs. A green meadow with horses and a duckpond extends behind it. The bluish silhouette of the city on the horizon seems as other-worldly and immaterial as a Fata Morgana. From left to right, one recognizes the towers of the three largest churches of the city, the Marienkirche, the St. Nikolai Cathedral, where Friedrich was christened, and the Jacobikirche. One of the medieval gates of the city is found exactly at the central axis of the painting. Behind this starts the Lange Straße, which extends from west to east through the city to the market, and on which Friedrich's family home was also found.

Meadow near Greifswald **ca. 1821/22**
Oil on canvas 34.5 × 48.3 cm
Hamburger Kunsthalle

H → Harbor

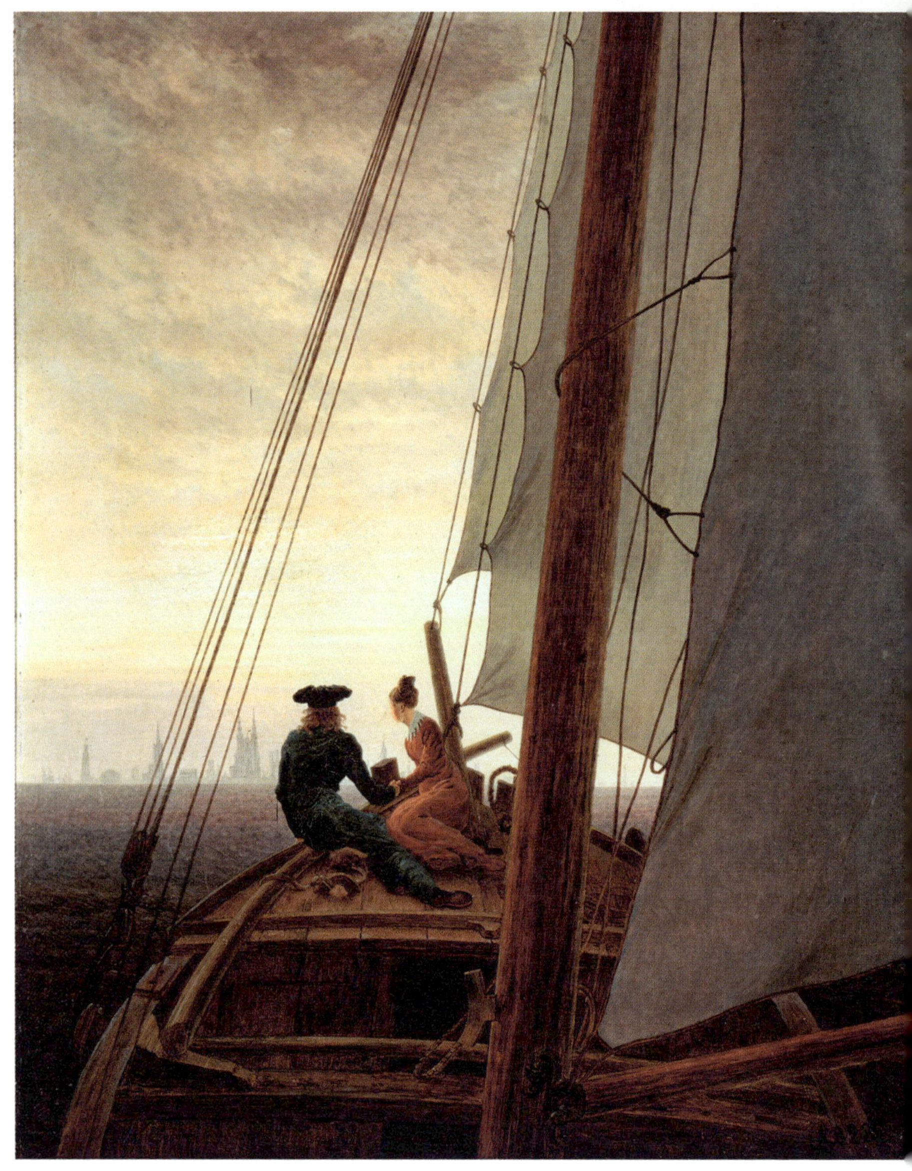

Friedrich grew up in a port city →Greifswald and was thus able to find inspiration for his maritime paintings not only in art history, for example, from the French painter Claude Joseph Vernet (1714–1789), but also in his immediate surroundings. Many sketches that later flowed into the compositions of his seascapes show motifs from the harbor of Greifswald. His harbor view,→p. 42 which originated in 1815–16, could be seen in 1816 in an exhibition in the Dresden Academy of Arts. Following this presentation, Friedrich was made a member of the Academy, which went hand in hand with a modest annual salary of 150 thaler; the painting was—like *Monk by the Sea* →Young's *Night-Thoughts* and *Abbey in the Oakwood*—acquired by the Prussian King Frederick William III.

Friedrich sailed into the "harbor of marriage" in 1818 with his marriage to Caroline Bommer.→Bride His painting *On the Sailing Ship* (around 1818–20) is a reminder of this event. A couple gazes at a seemingly almost immaterial, ideal city on the distant, misty horizon, where several church towers can be seen. The longing of the couple is therefore, according to a common reading, oriented less to worldly happiness than, in keeping with the Christian tradition, to the beyond and a life after death.[15] However, the destination of the journey remains blurred; a universal feeling of wanderlust and a shared mood of departure is predominant.

On the Sailing Ship **ca. 1818–1820**
Oil on canvas 71 × 56 cm
Hermitage, St. Petersburg

View of a Harbor **1815/16**
Oil on canvas 91 × 71 cm
Gemäldesammlung,
Stiftung Preußische Schlösser und Gärten

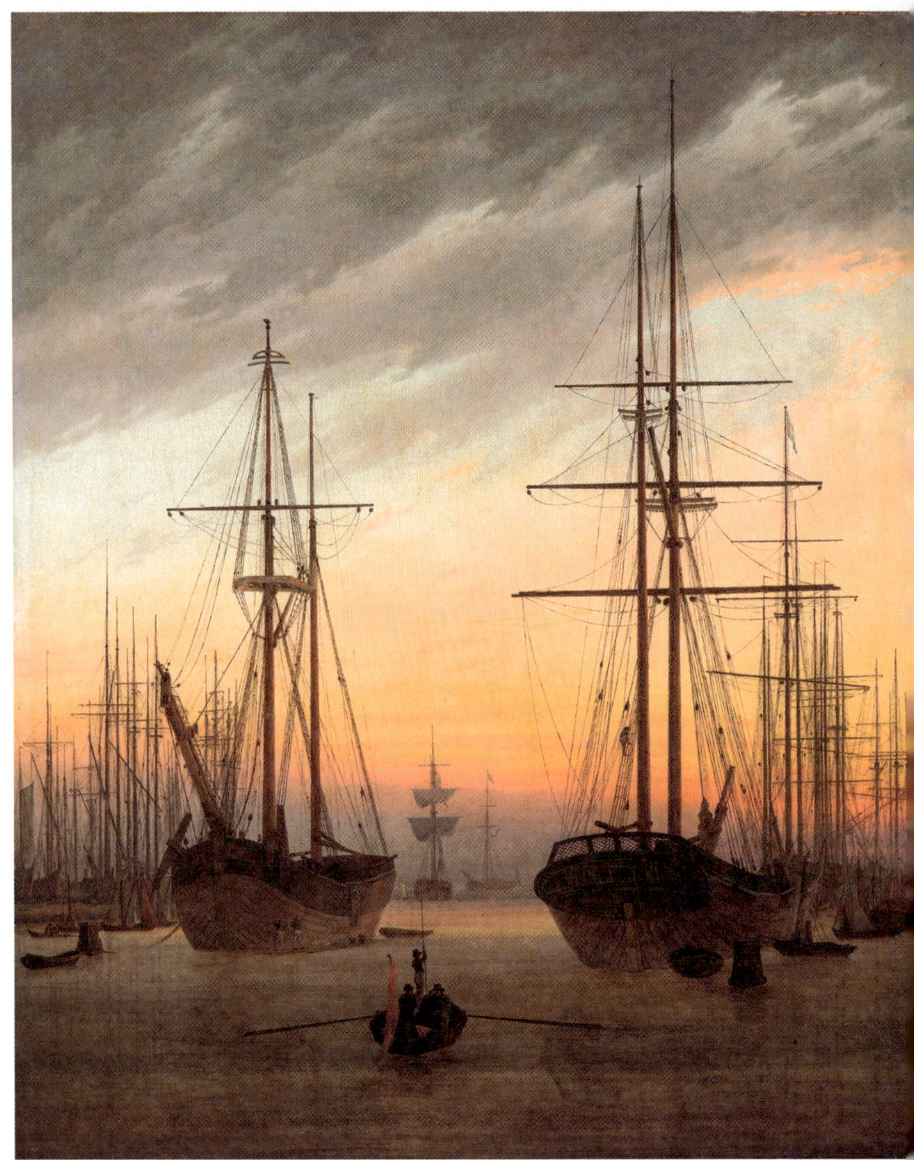

I→ Inwardness

In German, the word *Innerlichkeit* (inwardness) is first found in 1779 with the poet Friedrich Gottlieb Klopstock (1724–1803), whose writings Friedrich may have been familiar with, and a short time later with Johann Wolfgang von Goethe (1749–1832), who was one of Friedrich's early supporters.[16] Friedrich was also committed to inwardness and made an artistic program of it: "The painter should not merely paint what he sees in front of him, but instead also what he sees in himself. However, if he sees nothing in himself, he should also dispense with painting what he sees in front of him."[17] This statement points out how his paintings can be seen: as views of his inner world.

Friedrich's so-called "window sepias" (around 1805–06) show views from his two studio windows on the Elbe. They are composed according to the principle of the golden ratio.→ Under Construction In that Friedrich subordinates the window sepias, but also later works, to a system, he emphasizes that he is not merely painting what he sees in front of him—even if the view onto the river and the opposite shore initially appears realistic. Everyday things like the key hanging on the wall, the letter addressed to Friedrich lying on the windowsill, or the scissors should also be understood as bearers of meaning; the scissors could thus refer to the *Goldener Schnitt* (golden ratio, but in German literally "golden cut") and the key to the *verschlüsselt* (encoded or encrypted, but in German literally "keyed") meaning of the pair of drawings.

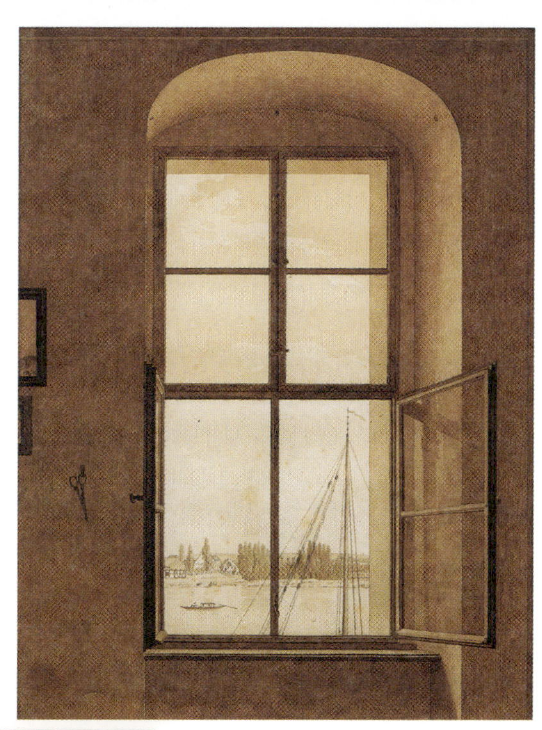

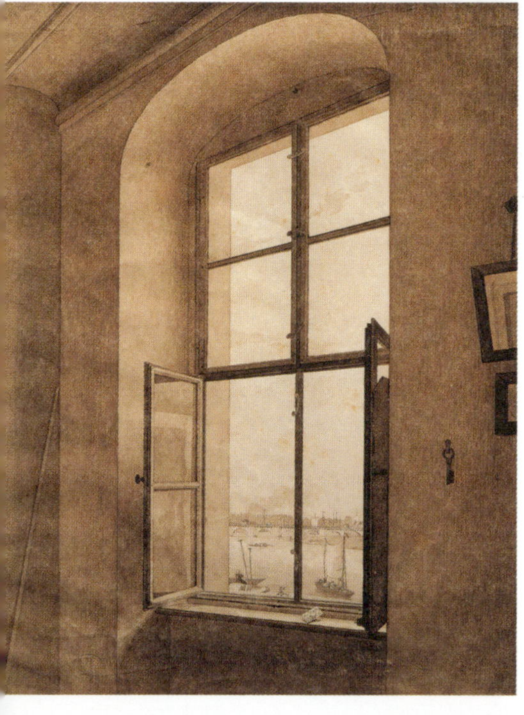

However, the window sepias show one thing quite clearly, namely that a fissure passes through the artist and through his perspective. This is because, while the right window is represented almost frontally, the left window is captured in an oblique view. At the right edge of the left drawing and at the left edge of the right drawing one sees, respectively, a part of a framed, quasi divided mirror, in the right half of which the artist has placed a self-portrait. The pair of images shows Friedrich as a "dividuum," as divisible, possibly even as broken; it at the same time demonstrates that he was already prepared at the beginning of his career to deviate from traditional standpoints and aesthetic conventions.

View from the Artist's Atelier, Right Window **ca. 1805/06**
Pencil and pen with brown wash 31.4 × 23.5 cm
Österreichische Galerie Belvedere, Vienna

View from the Artist's Atelier, Left Window **ca. 1805/06**
Pencil and pen with brown wash 31.2 × 23.7 cm
Österreichische Galerie Belvedere, Vienna

J → Jeers

In July 1816, Friedrich wrote a letter to the painter Johann Ludwig Lund in Rome, whom he knew from his student years in Copenhagen. He asked Lund to send his regards to several artist colleagues who were residing in the Italian city of art—"only not Chamberlain von Ramdohr."[18] Friedrich apparently had reason to bear a grudge.

The catalyst for the feud, which has gone down in art history as the "Ramdohr Dispute," was Friedrich's painting *The Cross in the Mountains*, also known as the *Tetschen Altar*, which was as ambitious as it was controversial. The second title is a little misleading. This is because, although Friedrich had originally planned the painting with the complex frame he had designed himself for a chapel, it never served as an altarpiece.

Its exhibition history began at Christmas of 1808, when Friedrich staged it effectively in his Dresden workshop in a darkened room for a select public. Friedrich, who was born in Swedish Pomerania, had actually intended the painting for his much-esteemed Swedish King Gustav IV Adolph, whose Protestant beliefs he shared. However, following the invasion by Napoleonic troops and the end of Gustav's rule, it became impossible to hand over the artwork.[19] Count Franz Anton von Thun-Hohenstein was thus able to acquire it for his wife Theresia Maria. The painting was found in their castle in North Bohemian Tetschen, now Děčín, until 1921. However, not in the chapel, but instead in the

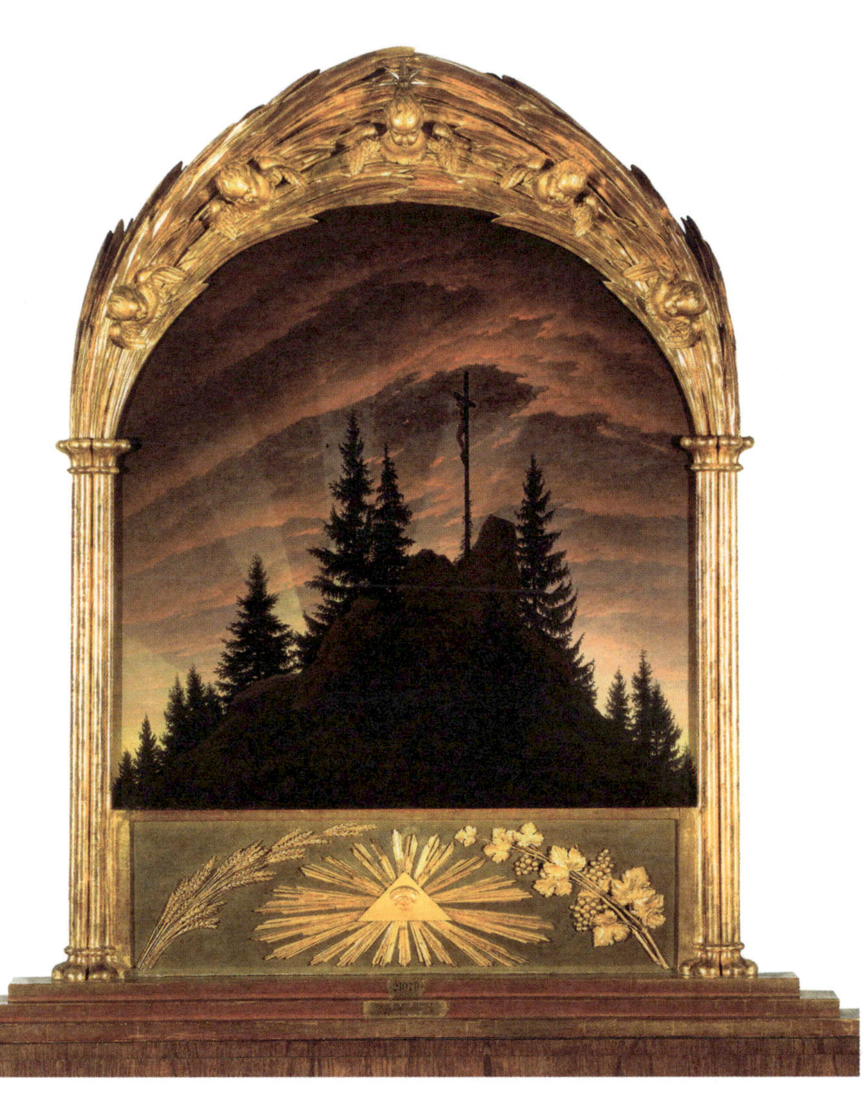

bedchamber of the Countess, together with an engraving after Raphael's *Sistine Madonna* (1512–13). The oft reproduced work of the Italian Renaissance master found its way in 1753 into the Dresden collection →Dresden of the Saxon Elector Augustus III; in 1921, *The Cross in the Mountains* was also acquired for the Gemäldegalerie in Dresden.

While the work was removed from the public view soon after it was created, it was broadly debated in art criticism. In 1809, the Prussian diplomat and artist Wilhelm Basilius von Ramdohr formulated a fundamental criticism of Friedrich's unconventional pictorial invention: he found fault with offences against the rules of perspective and optics; he criticized that the time of day of the scene was not clearly recognizable, and saw a mysticism at work "that is now creeping in everywhere and fulminates against us like a narcotic vapor from art and science, from philosophy and religion!"[20]

He was particularly appalled by the fact that Friedrich transgressed against the academic genre boundaries between landscape painting and religious art: "It is in fact true presumption when landscape painting tries to sneak into the churches and to crawl onto altars." The artist, who was at that time at the beginning of his career, countered self-confidently: had "Friedrich made use of the crutches of art and not shown the presumption to want to walk on his own two feet, Chamberlain von Ramdohr would never have been disturbed from his rest."[21] The Prussian diplomat proved capable of self-reflection and revised his judgment publicly: "My words will be forgotten, and his works will live on."[22]

The Cross in the Mountains (Tetschen Altar) 1807/08
Oil on canvas 115 × 110.5 cm
Galerie Neue Meister, Staatliche Kunstsammlungen Dresden

K → Kersting

Depictions of artists at work can be viewed as programmatic. They not only provide information on technical questions, but also visualize the self-comprehension and the conception of art of those represented. This also applies for the paintings of Georg Friedrich Kersting, which depict Friedrich in his Dresden studio.→Dresden →p. 55 Kersting was a friend of Friedrich, and had, like him, studied in Copenhagen and undertaken hikes with him; he is said to have even helped him with several representations of figures. This familiarity between the painters makes Kersting's studio paintings particularly insightful.

The first version of Kersting's painting shows Friedrich at work on a landscape painting depicting a waterfall. Daylight shines through a window, its bottom shutters closed; the top section shows only a section of sky behind the cruciform glazing bars, which are reminiscent of the Christian symbol of the cross. Corresponding with the blue of the sky behind the window cross is a glass vessel on a worktable containing a conspicuously brilliant, light blue pigment—the material substance of the painted sky and perhaps a reference to a Romantic motif of longing, the blue flower of the poet Novalis. Two palettes hang on the wall and on the completely closed shutters of the second window, but also a T-square and a set square—an indication that Friedrich often constructed his compositions according to geometric principles.

The second version of Kersting's studio painting appears to once again intensify the statement of the first. The image section has been reduced; there is no longer a door seen at the left edge and the right window is also cut off. Friedrich isn't working at the easel but is instead standing behind a chair, looking at his painting, of which we can see only the back. The barrenness of Friedrich's studio was described vividly by several visitors; for Wilhelm von Kügelgen in 1813, it was "of such absolute emptiness that [the poet] Jean Paul could have compared it with the disembowelled corpse of a dead prince."[23] Kersting's studio paintings thus appear on the one hand as realistic insights into Friedrich's workspace; at the same time, they visualize the conceptual character of Friedrich's painting, who confessed that he first saw his paintings "with the mental eye."

Georg Friedrich Kersting
Caspar David Friedrich in his Studio 1811
Oil on canvas 54 × 42 cm
Hamburger Kunsthalle

Georg Friedrich Kersting
Caspar David Friedrich in his Studio ca. 1812
Oil on canvas 53.5 × 41 cm
Alte Nationalgalerie, Staatliche Museen zu Berlin

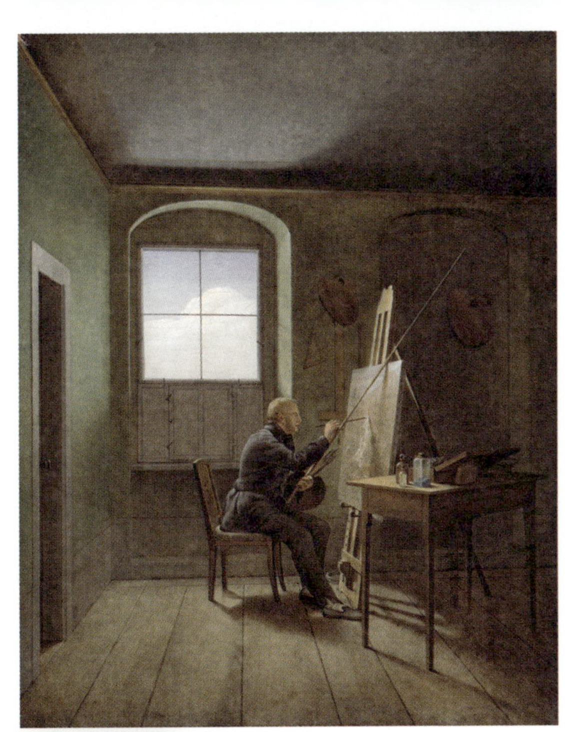

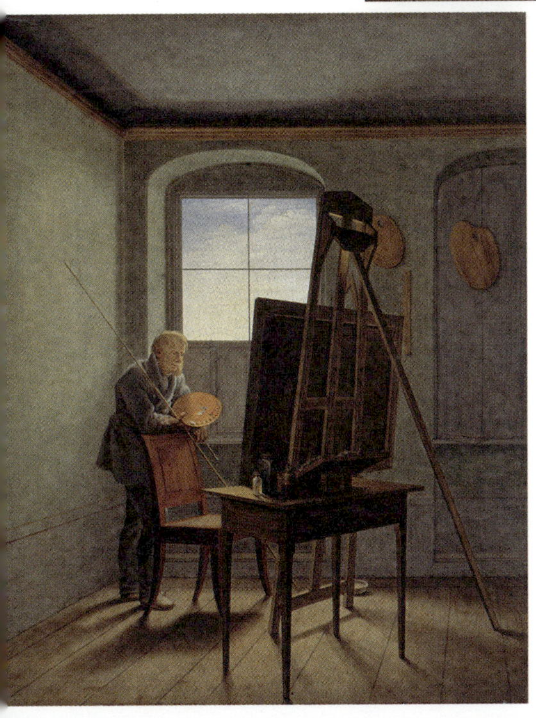

L → Last Generation

"Here is a man who has discovered the tragedy of the landscape," the French sculptor David d'Angers is said to have called out when he visited Caspar David Friedrich's studio in November 1834.[24] This oft-cited line can be understood such that Friedrich's landscapes triggered emotions like fear and pity in the public of the time. At the same time, one can also hear that his paintings are not naturalistic depictions of real landscapes, but instead artfully composed stagings.

Today, the perspective on real landscapes often applies to entirely concrete tragedies—the melting ice of the Antarctic, destructive floods or, devastating forest fires. Conversely, climate change increasingly also influences our perspective on art. *Everybody Talks About the Weather* was the title of an exhibition in 2023 in the Fondazione Prada in Venice, a city that is obviously existentially threatened by rising sea levels. In order to point to this danger, no original artworks were shown on the ground floor of the Palazzo Ca' Corner della Regina on the Grand Canal, but instead only reproductions, including Friedrich's catastrophic *The Sea of Ice* (around 1823–24).→pp. 68–69

Wanderer above the Sea of Fog (around 1817–18) →p. 59 is another famous painting by Friedrich that has been repeatedly placed into new contexts and experienced numerous reinterpretations.→Wanderer In March 2023, two activists of Letzte Generation (Last Generation) chose this painting in the Hamburger Kunsthalle as the backdrop for a previously announced action. To this purpose they invented a "realistic version" (L.G.) of the motif, in which this wanderer is not looking at a foggy mountain landscape in Saxon Switzerland, but instead at a flaming inferno full of billowing smoke—the "Wanderer in the Sea of Fire." The attempt to glue this version over Friedrich's painting behind glass was foiled by security. The activists then laid it in front of the original on the floor and scattered it with ashes originating from the forest fires of the summer of 2022 in Saxon Switzerland. That the destruction of landscapes through fires and droughts, floods and the melting of glaciers would also have shaken Friedrich goes without question.

Wanderer above the Sea of Fog **ca. 1817/18**
Oil on canvas 94.8 × 74.8 cm
Hamburger Kunsthalle

Film stills from the action in the Hamburger Kunsthalle:
Wanderer in the Sea of Fire **2023**
https://twitter.com/AufstandLastGen/status/1637473245828923392?lang=de

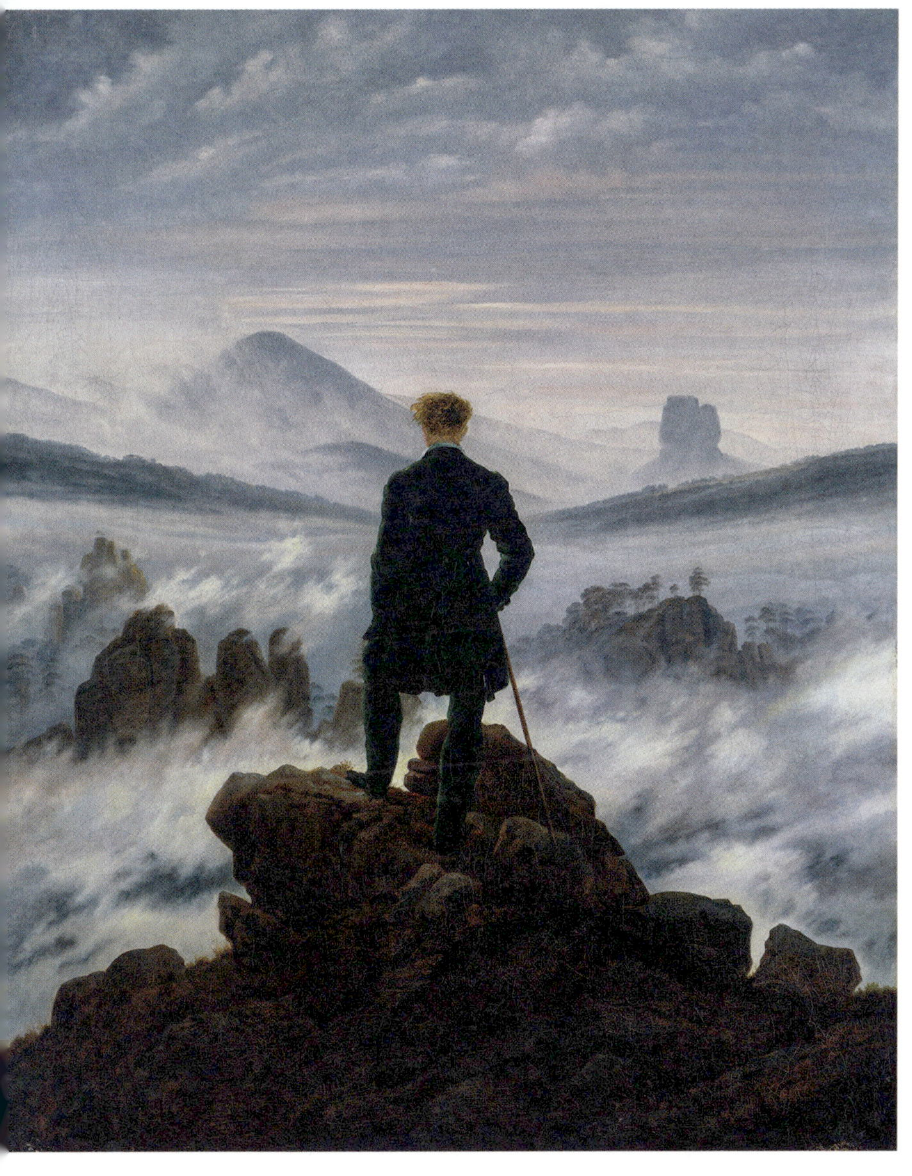

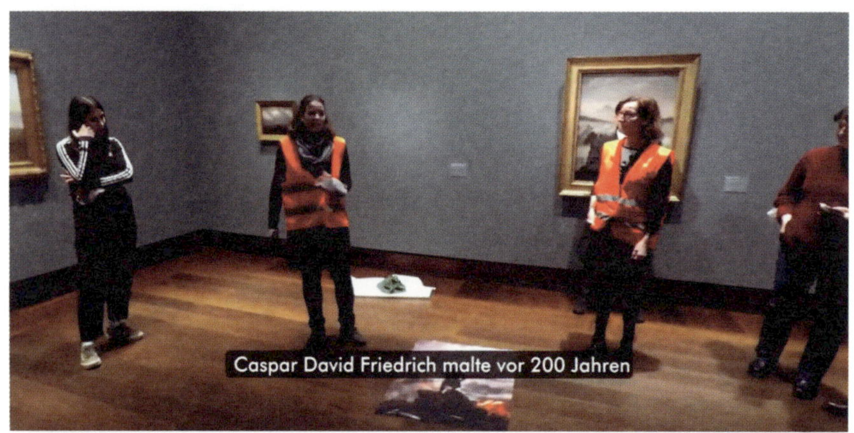
Caspar David Friedrich malte vor 200 Jahren

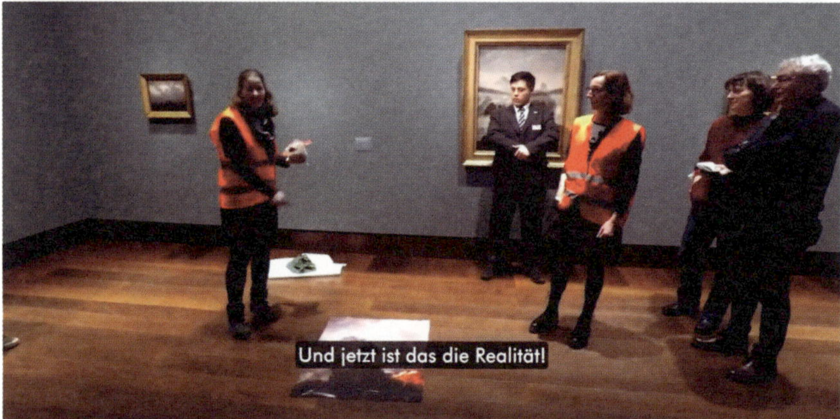
Und jetzt ist das die Realität!

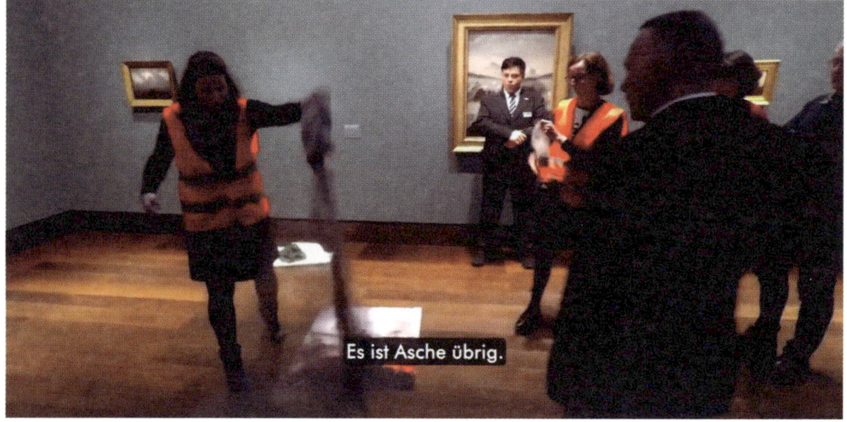
Es ist Asche übrig.

M → Moon

"A country road. A tree. Evening." An iconic theater play of the modern era begins with this scene description; Samuel Beckett's *Waiting for Godot*, the French version of which premiered in 1953 in Paris. Toward the end of the first act, the two main figures contemplate the moon which is "pale for weariness" of "climbing heaven and gazing on the likes of us."

It is no coincidence that these quotations are remotely reminiscent of a night painting by Friedrich. Beckett traveled through Germany in 1936–37, where the National Socialist dictatorship had ruled since 1933, and also visited important museums like the Hamburger Kunsthalle and the Alte Pinakothek in Munich during his stay; in February 1937, he even visited the Dresden Zwinger several times. There, according to a diary entry from February 14, he developed a "pleasant predilection for 2 tiny languid men in his landscapes, as in the little moon landscape."[25]

In addition to the painting in Dresden, two further versions of the work are found in the Nationalgalerie in Berlin and in The Metropolitan Museum in New York. Two back-figures stand close to one another on a path descending diagonally from left to right; an uprooted, dead oak and a rock supporting it lean in the opposite direction. The two figures gaze at the moon at the center of the composition. One of the men is wearing old German dress, an identifying mark of the

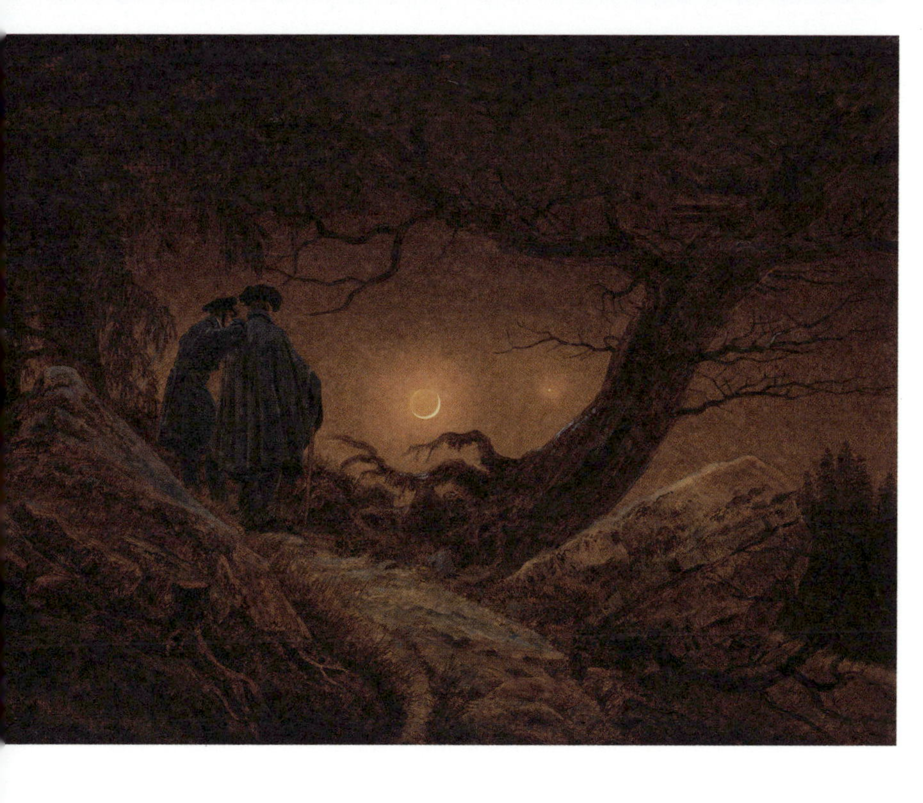

national liberal bourgeoisie calling for rights of freedom, which was subject to hard repression by the ruling princes following the Vienna Congress of 1814–15. One political interpretation of the painting therefore sees the moon as standing for change, with the dark present soon to make way for a bright future.[26] Perhaps Beckett had intuitively perceived a slight resistance in Friedrich's painting, which stood in contrast with the repulsive clangor and the brutal political conditions of the country he found himself in. In any case, Friedrich's night painting was for Beckett "the only kind of romantic still tolerable, the bémolisé."[27]

Two Men Contemplating the Moon **1819/20**
Oil on canvas 33 × 44.5 cm
Galerie Neue Meister, Staatliche Kunstsammlungen Dresden

N → Northwest Passage

With the painting *The Sea of Ice* (around 1823–24), Friedrich took up a motif that has a rich tradition: the shipwreck. He had produced three oil sketches of ice floes on the Elbe in the winter of 1820–21. These detail studies of the rare natural spectacle found their way into the painting; the composition itself is, however, a product of the power of imagination and is today perhaps reminiscent of the special effects of the film *The Day After Tomorrow* (2004), in which a climate disaster covers large parts of the earth with ice.

In Friedrich's painting, the sunken sailing vessel is still only a disappearing remainder, ground between slabs of ice towering up like pyramids. In the background is a polar landscape with similar floe formations extending to the horizon. The overcast sky only clears up in the middle of the top edge of the painting.

The Sea of Ice was apparently a flop with its contemporary public. As with the *Tetschen Altar (The Cross in the Mountains)* from years before, here, too, it was criticized,→Jeers that the perspective was "not truly motivated." In addition, it was said that the "ice floes as main subject" were not an appropriate motif, and another person admitted that the painting was beautiful, but she didn't want "to always have to look at it."[28] Friedrich had every reason to shudder in the face of such a lack of understanding, and *The Sea of Ice* in fact remained unsold until the death of the artist.

Nevertheless, the painting has been subject to numerous interpretations. Friedrich's younger brother Johann Christoffer drowned in 1787 rescuing Caspar David from the moat in Greifswald; this decisive experience is often put forward as one of the reasons for Friedrich's tendency to melancholy and his intensive preoccupation with themes like death and mourning. Read politically, *The Sea of Ice* might function as an allegory of the petrified societal conditions following the Vienna Congress of 1814–15. A concrete impetus for the motif of a ship gone down in the pack ice could have been the expeditions of the British naval officer William Edward Parry (1790–1855), who searched for the Northwest Passage between the Atlantic and the Pacific Oceans in the Arctic.

The Sea of Ice **ca. 1823/24**
Oil on canvas 96.7 × 126.9 cm
Hamburger Kunsthalle

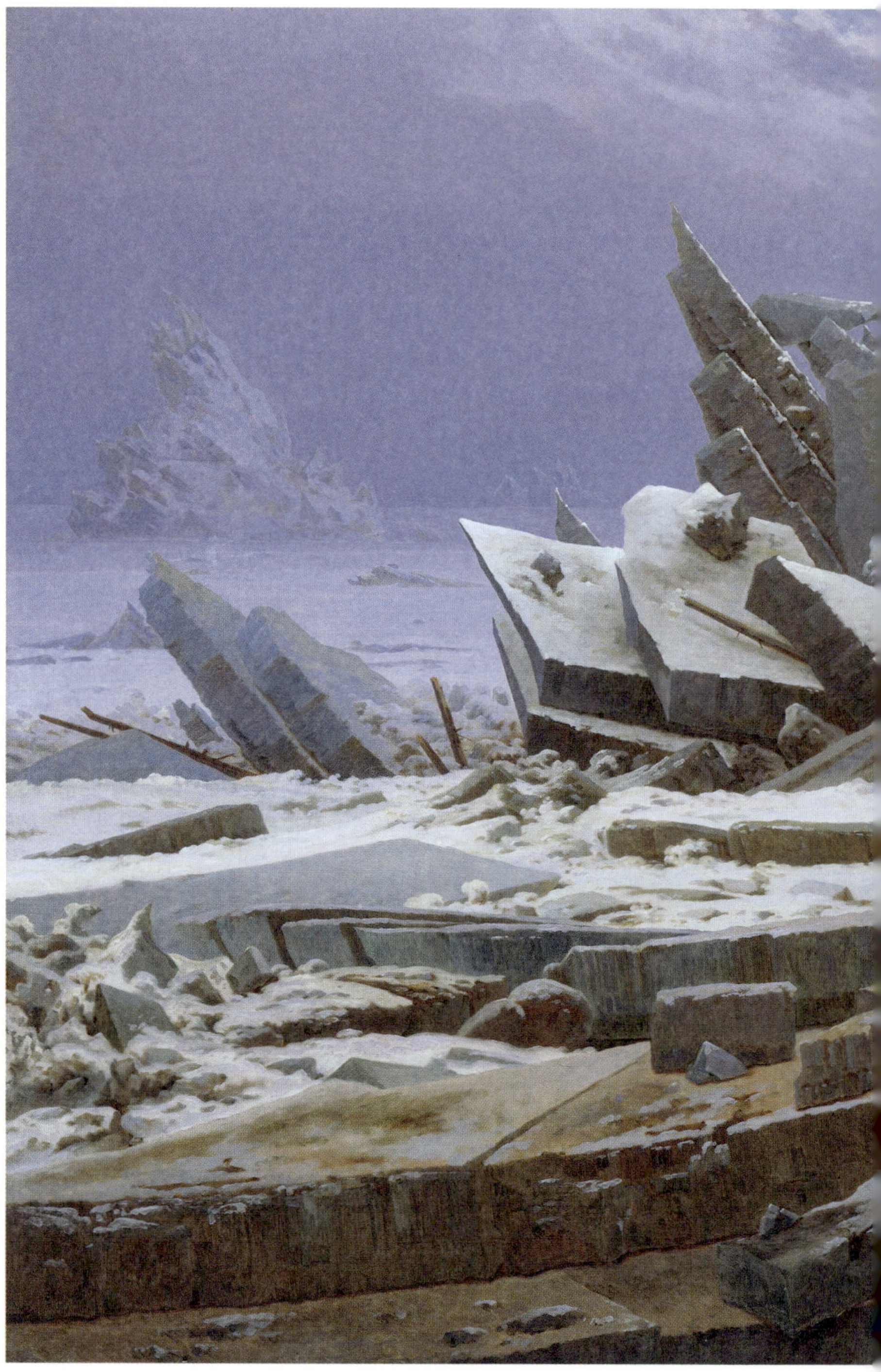

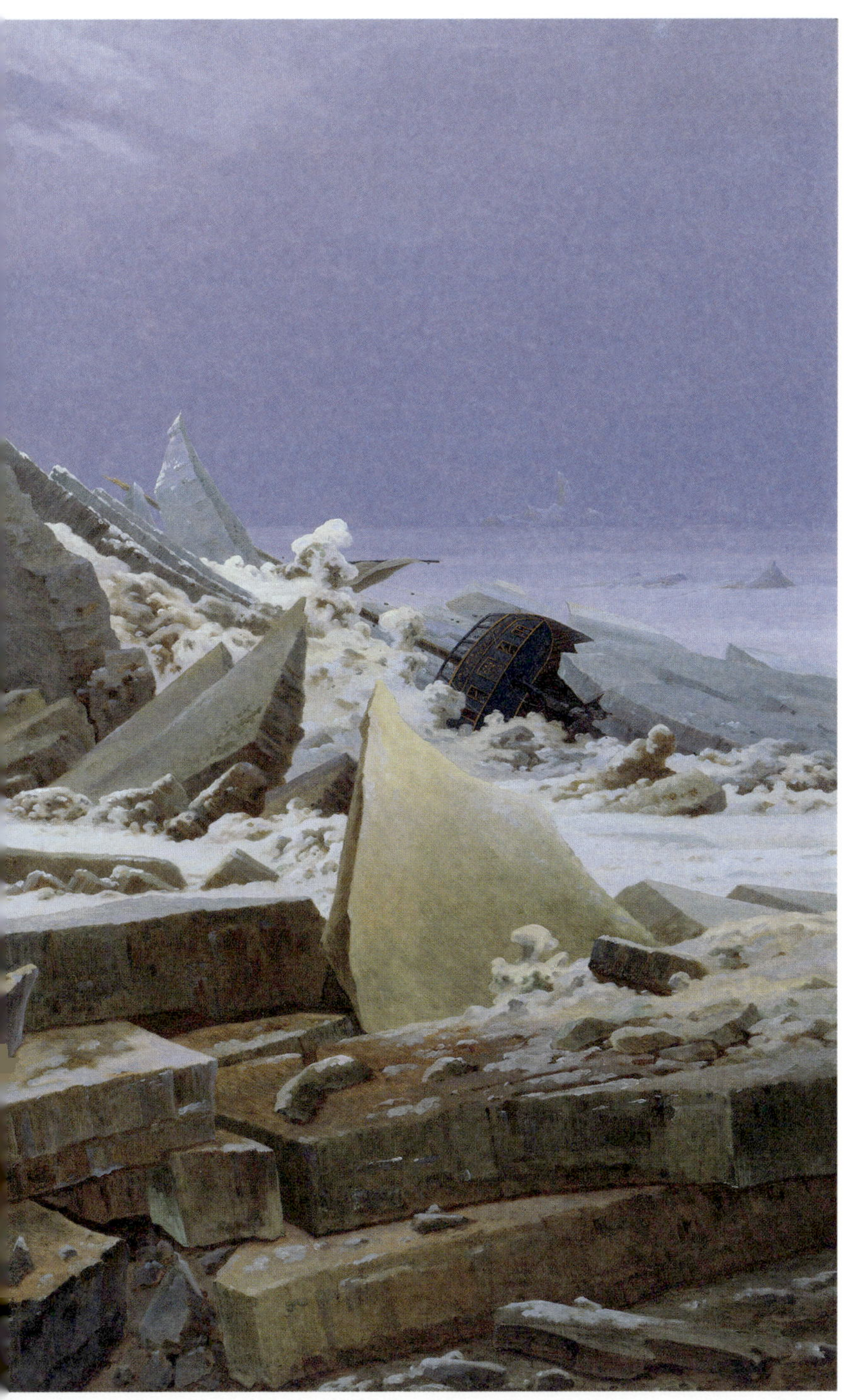

o → Owl

Among the latest additions from Friedrich's catalogue raisonné is the *Owl in a Tree.*[29] →p.72 After the French sculptor David d'Angers → Last Generation had visited Friedrich in November 1834 in his Dresden studio,→Kersting he wrote: "Only after being asked many times did Friedrich pull out a few works for us, including a painting representing a tree. It has no leaves whatsoever; an owl is perched on one of its branches, and the diffuse light of the moon illuminates the background. No ground in which the tree could be rooted. An effect bordering on reverie."[30] A "small painting (*Owl in a Tree* by Friedrich)" is listed in d'Angers's estate inventory, which remained the property of his descendants until 1878. The whereabouts of the painting were subsequently unknown until it turned up again in 2011 on the website of a French auction house. The batch originated from an estate sale, estimated value "80 to 100 Euro." An art trade mystery followed, until the unusual painting changed owners for 6.5 million euros.

In fact, Friedrich created several sepia drawings in the mid-1830s, a few years prior to his death, in which owls play a vital role—not because he had turned to animal studies in his late work, but instead likely due to the symbolic significance of the nocturnal bird as a messenger of death and memento mori as well as being a symbol of wisdom. In Friedrich's sheets, an owl literally flies into the faces of the viewers or is perched puffed up in a Gothic window, on a graveyard

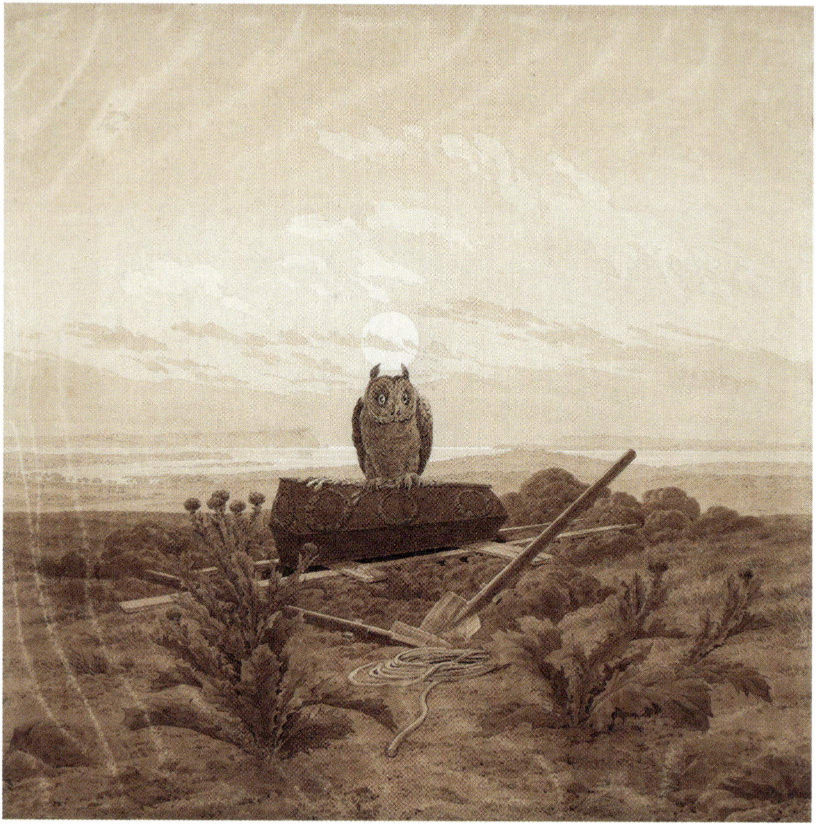

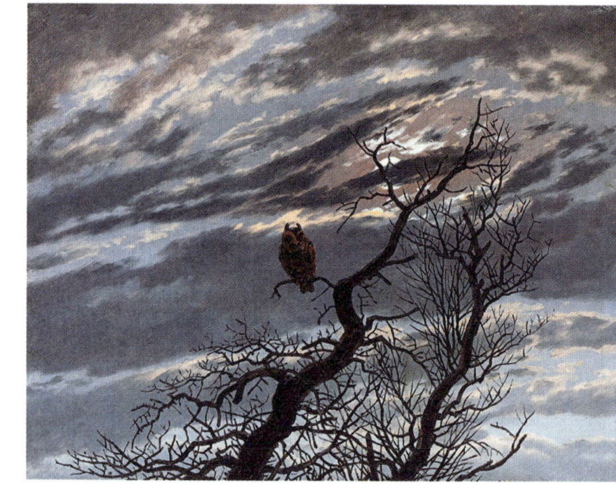

cross, on the shovel of a gravedigger, or as an oversized figure on a casket. Besides these sepia drawings, there are only a few works of Friedrich in which a figure directs its gaze at a counterpart outside of the painting—namely his self-portraits.→Frontispiece It seems as if the artist—who some contemporaries saw as a *Kauz* (an old coot, oddball, but also a German variant for owl) or peculiar—could identify with the owl.

Landscape with Grave, Coffin, and Owl **ca. 1836/37**
Pencil on velin with brown wash 38.5 × 38.4 cm
Hamburger Kunsthalle, Kupferstichkabinett

Owl in a Tree **ca. 1834**
Oil on canvas 25.2 × 31.1 cm
Private Collection

P → Politics

"As in art, so he also was in life," wrote Carl Gustav Carus (1789–1869) a quarter of a century after Friedrich's death in his *Lebenserinnerungen und Denkwürdigkeiten* (1865–66), "of strict lawfulness, rectitude, and seclusiveness—German through and through. Never would he even have attempted to learn one of the foreign modern languages."[31]

Carus, born in Leipzig, was a doctor and artist. He had lived in Dresden since 1814, was friends with Friedrich as of 1818 and was initially also his student in landscape painting. In the mid-1820s, however, the two different characters began to grow apart. The ambitious and worldly Carus was increasingly successful in both careers, while Friedrich had grown increasingly marginalized due to his artistic and social nonconformism, as well as his being weakened by health crises.

The characterization of Friedrich as "German through and through" sounds ominous today. His preferred motifs, such as fir and oak trees, his predilection for prehistoric megalithic barrows, but also his expressly political, patriotic painting *Hutten's Tomb* (around 1823–24) → Zittau Mountains were coopted by the National Socialist regime and exploited for propaganda purposes. Friedrich was declared the forefather of the *Friedrichdeutsche* (Frederician Germans), his clouds as *Rassenwolken* (race clouds) and his trees as *Seelenbäume* (soul trees).[32] The centenary of the death of the artist in 1940 served the purpose of justifying and ideologically exalting the destruction of the Second World War with his paintings of Gothic ruins. The two hundredth anniversary of his birth in 1974 provided the occasion to rediscover the artist, but also to throw light on the history of the *völkisch* instrumentalization of his art and to dismantle the *Weiheaura* (aura of consecration) surrounding his work.

Q → Quistorp

With Johann Gottfried Quistorp (1755–1835), the young Caspar David Friedrich had been learning since about 1790 what his teacher referred to as the "mechanical aspect of art," which "is so difficult to bring forth from oneself"[33]—drawing from references and plaster casts of ancient sculptures. Quistorp was an architect and a drawing teacher at the University of Greifswald, and Friedrich began taking part in his public lessons as a sixteen-year-old. Quistorp also possessed an extensive collection of freehand drawings, copperplate engravings, and paintings, so that his pupils received insight into European art history despite the Pomeranian isolation.

Friedrich's participation in Quistorp's lessons ended in 1794, but the contact between the two artists was maintained. Quistorp helped make it possible for Friedrich to continue his training at the renowned academy of arts in Copenhagen, and both went hiking together, including on Rügen and in the vicinity of Greifswald.→ Greifswald Friedrich drew the barrow of Gützkow on such an occasion in 1802. These prehistoric stone settings, especially prevalent in northern Europe, inspired many artists to images and texts in the eighteenth and early nineteenth centuries. They could stand for an overcome heathenish prehistory but were also celebrated as symbols of the resilience of an ancient culture viewed as typically "Nordic" and as monuments to past greatness. One sometimes referred to them as *Hünenbetten* (long barrows, but literally "giants'

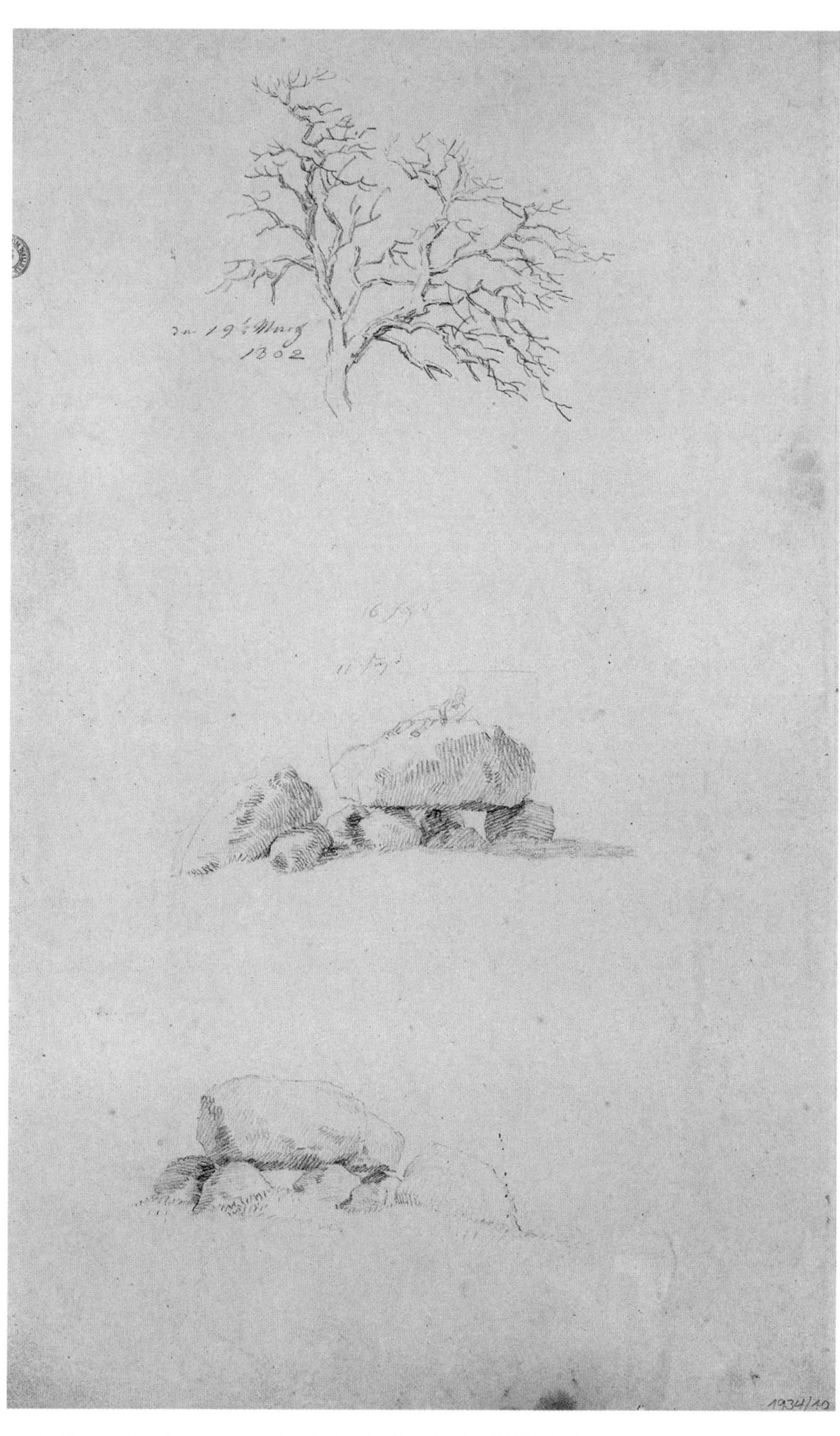
1802
1934/10

beds," and this is how Friedrich interpreted them in several images, representing them as couches of a kind.→p. 79 Friedrich's—and Quistorp's—approach to the impressive giant stones thereby bears witness to a certain coziness and appears free of exaggerated awe. "When Friedrich drew the barrow," his one-time drawing teacher wrote, "I lay above on the capstone and smoked a pipe, and that's how he included me in his study book."[34]

Barrow with a Man Lying on It and Tree Study **March 19, 1802**
Pencil on paper 36.3 × 22.6 cm
Wallraf-Richartz-Museum & Fondation Corboud, Department of Drawings and Prints, Cologne

R → Rearview Figure

The rearview figure (*Rückenfigur*), whose back is toward the viewer, was not Friedrich's invention. However, he used it and developed it further so idiosyncratically that it has become a defining feature of his art. Friedrich was probably already familiar with historical paintings with rearview figures from the collection of his first drawing teacher Quistorp.→ Quistorp In any case, the sketch of a *Male Nude from Behind*, which still reveals technical difficulties with the motif, originates from these years of instruction between 1790 and 1794.

One of his early, famous rearview figures is the *Monk By the Sea* (around 1808–10), who can also be seen as a proxy for the artist.→ pp. 110–11 The authors Clemens Brentano and Achim von Arnim wrote an amusing series of gallery conversations of fictitious viewers revolving around the painting. There, the remark is made that the artist should instead have "stretched out the monk sleeping or praying or looking, prone in all modesty, so that he does not spoil the prospect for spectators, who are obviously more impressed by the broad sea than with the little Capuchin."[35] → Young's *Night-Thoughts*

A decisive function of the rearview figure is thus already registered. It guides the gaze into the painting and at the same time blocks it—it "spoils the prospect," as Brentano and Von Arnim formulated ironically but accurately. That which the rearview figure sees—when it, as it often does with Friedrich, stands in the central

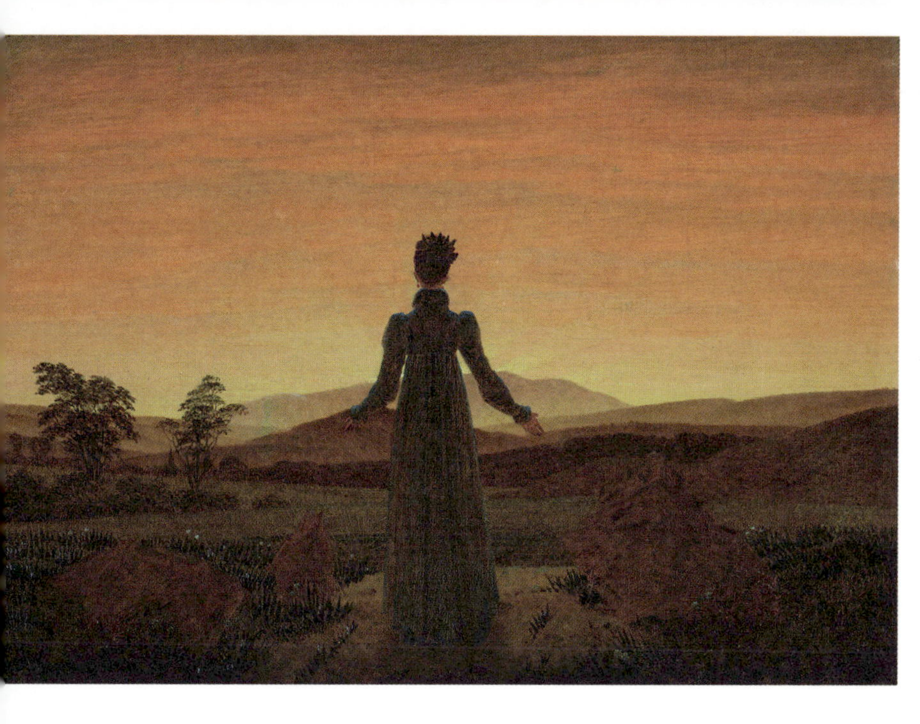

axis of the painting—remains concealed from the gaze of viewers before the painting, therefore appealing to their power of imagination. It is the proxy and identification figure for viewers, but also generates a distance between them and the represented landscape. At the same time, the rearview figure embodies the experience and the pleasure of viewing itself, the contemplative immersion into a landscape and endless space.

Woman before the Setting **(or: *Rising*) *Sun* ca. 1818**
Oil on canvas 22 × 30.5 cm
Museum Folkwang, Essen

s → Sepia

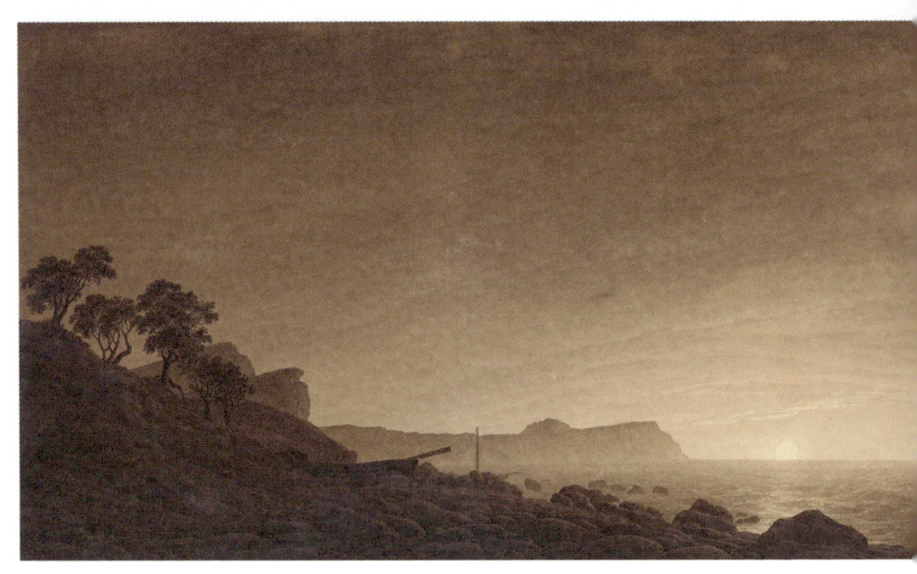

Sepia was to some extent a Dresden "local color." The Dresden-born →Dresden painter Jakob Crescenz Seydelmann (1750–1829) is viewed as the first painter to use the glandular secretion of the octopus to produce monochrome copies of famous paintings in original size.[36] The Swiss Adrian Zingg (1734–1816), professor for landscape drawing at the Dresden Academy, was also a master in this technique. He went wandering with his colleague Anton Graff (1736–1813), for example, in the Elbe Sandstone Mountains, which reminded the two wanderers →Wanderer of their home region, the Swiss Jura Mountains. They are also credited with coining the term "Sächsische Schweiz" (Saxon Switzerland).

Friedrich began to work with sepia in around 1800. Its use marks the transition between Friedrich as draughtsman and painter. And so, as the Swiss Zingg found motifs for his landscape representations in a region that reminded him of his origin, Friedrich dedicated several of his most impressive sepias to views of Rügen. In 1801 and 1802, he undertook at least three long hiking excursions on the Baltic Sea island off the Pomeranian coast. These resulted in drawings of prominent sights, which had at that time also become attractions for tourists, such as the steep chalk cliffs of Stubbenkammer and Cape Arkona.[37] Only several years later did Friedrich translate his sketches produced on location into large-format sepias like *View of Arkona with Rising Moon* (around 1805–06).

Friedrich produced the extraordinarily nuanced representation of an evening landscape, which appears to light up from within itself, from the dark brown sepia ink. At the same time, he here begins to construct his compositions according to strict rules.[38] →Under Construction The mast of a boat lying on the shore becomes apparent discreetly but unmistakably at the vertical center of the picture and slightly intersects the horizon line of the chalk cliff.

View of Arkona with Rising Moon **ca. 1805/06**
Pencil and brown ink 60.9 × 100 cm
Albertina, Vienna

T→ Transparent

Friedrich was a master of suggestive light moods. His *View of Arkona with Rising Moon* (around 1805–06) →p. 86 or the light bath of *Woman before the Setting* (or: *Rising*) *Sun* (around 1818) →p. 83 appear to be illuminated from within. Toward the end of his career, he even went as far as to also experiment with real light. Friedrich's transparent paintings are a special case among his painting pairs. While the latter are two individual works, the transparent works are painted both on the front and on the back and can—similar to a slide or film material—be activated by real light and transformed into a landscape in the morning or the evening depending upon the lighting. In this way, not only the *product*, but also the *process* of nature is visualized.[39]

Friedrich even hoped to expand a group of transparent paintings, of which only three draft drawings have survived, into a kind of total artwork with musical accompaniment. The drafts represent allegories of secular, religious, and celestial music; they show a lute player and a guitarist in Gothic architecture, a harpist on a balcony against the background of a church, and a dreaming musician with a mandolin, above which three angels float in a posture of adoration. Buyer of the complicated installation was the later Tsar Alexander II in St. Petersburg. In a letter from December 12, 1835, to the State Counsellor Vasily Andreyevich Zhukovsky, Friedrich provided detailed instructions on how to set up and present the work. He held several

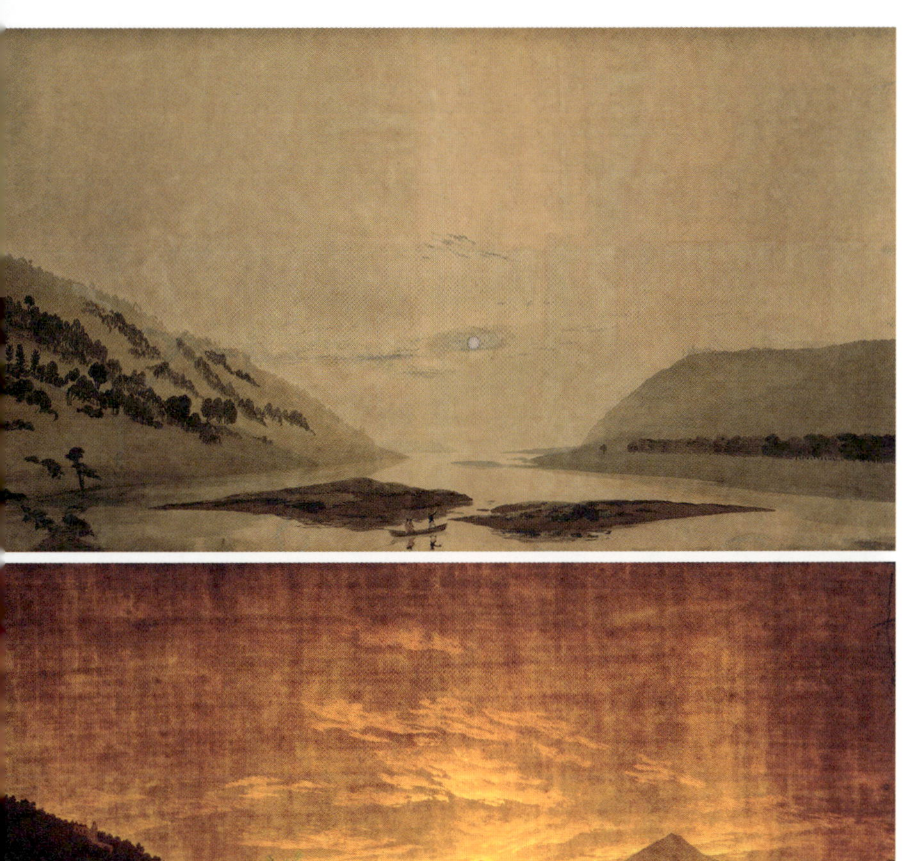

rehearsals to be necessary for the coordination between the alternating lighting and the performance of the music and was entirely aware of the difficulties that his novel work method made necessary; "it of course cannot proceed . . . quite as smoothly as viewing the oil paintings," he conceded.[40]

Mountainous River Landscape in the Morning
(View of the Front in Impinging Light) ca. 1830–1835
Watercolor and ink on transparent paper 74 × 124 cm
Staatliche Kunstsammlungen, Kassel

Mountainous River Landscape in the Morning
(View of the Front in Transmitted Light) ca. 1830–1835
Watercolor and ink on transparent paper 74 × 124 cm
Staatliche Kunstsammlungen, Kassel

U → Under Construction

Very few people will associate the terms "Romanticism" and "mathematics" straight away. The one is associated more with emotion, the other more with rationality. This may possibly already have applied for Friedrich's contemporaries. Pioneers of Romanticism like the poet Friedrich von Hardenberg, alias Novalis (1772–1801), or the philosopher and theologian Friedrich Schleiermacher (1768–1834), who visited Friedrich in his studio in 1810, however, strived to unify apparent contradictions. "To become one with the infinite amidst the finite" is Schleiermacher's definition of faith in his influential book *On Religion: Speeches to its Cultured Despisers* from 1799. And if the world, as Novalis formulated it, needs to be "romanticized" in order to recover its "original sense," then this romanticization could also be extended to mathematics.[41] The conception that the cosmos is ordered according to geometric principles can in fact be traced back to classical philosophy, and the Christian God was represented in the Middle Ages as the architect of the universe with a compass in his hand.

Against this background, it makes sense that Friedrich often constructed his pictorial worlds with the help of geometric principles. These also included the golden ratio, a division ratio of line segments that were referred to during the Renaissance as *divina proportione*, as "divine proportion."[42] This is also found in nature, for example, in the arrangements of the leaves

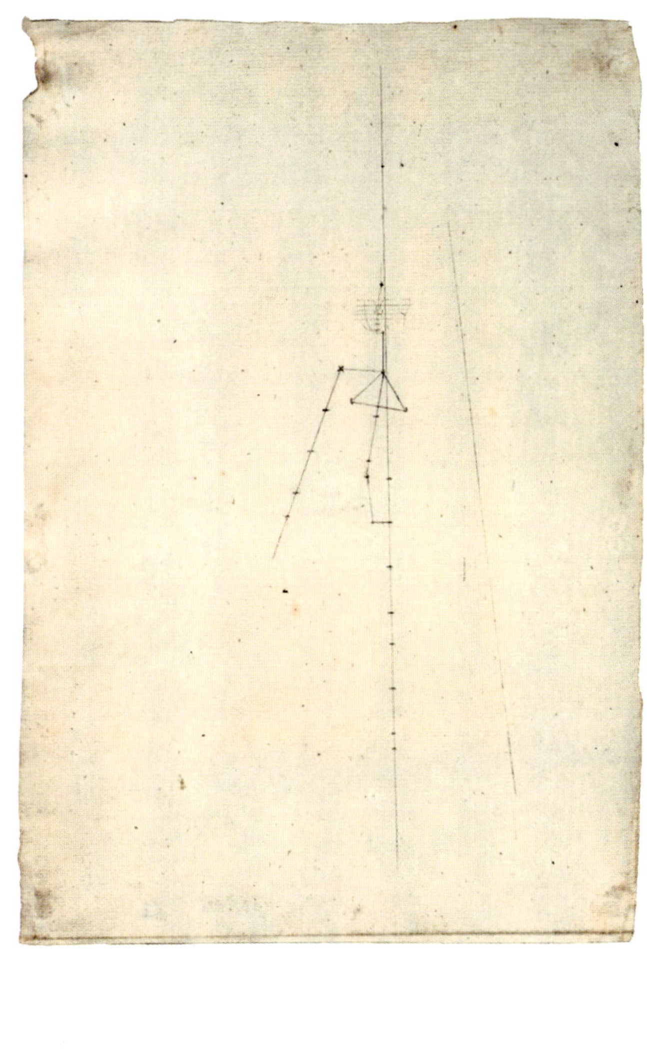

of some plants, and is often perceived as especially balanced and harmonious. An early example of Friedrich's use of the golden ratio is found in his window sepias.[→ p. 45] More easily recognizable is Friedrich's preference for symmetrical axes, for example, in *Woman before the Setting* (or: *Rising*) *Sun*,[→ p. 83] and for hyperbola, like in *The Large Enclosure near Dresden*.[→ pp. 20–21] Through the use of such design principles works were created in which everything appears to be meaningfully and almost magically at the right place.

Diagramme of a Nude **ca. 1790–1794**
Pencil on laid paper 20.1 × 19.9 cm
Pommersches Landesmuseum, Greifswald

v → **View**

With the *Woman at the Window* (1822),→p. 99 Friedrich returned to a motif that had already occupied him in two sepias →Sepia around 1805–06: the view out the window. It is presumed that the interior in the early window sepias →Inwardness and in *Woman at the Window* shows the studio of the artist. The family moved in 1820 following his marriage to Caroline Bommer →Bride and the birth of their first daughter, but the new apartment also had a view of the Elbe. The model for the *Woman at the Window* was Friedrich's wife. The motif of a back-figure at the window is an exception in his work—although or perhaps because window paintings have a long tradition in art history that Friedrich may have wanted to leave behind.

The contrast between interior and exterior world in this painting could hardly be greater. The subdued shades of green and brown of the wall and the shutters are also found in the dress of the back-figure; they belong to the same sphere to a certain extent. In contrast, the world beyond the window appears to be filled with attractive brightness; the alley on the opposite bank of the Elbe is flooded with light, the sky is light blue and traversed by small, white clouds. There is in fact not only one window in the painting, but rather two: the lower window, through which the woman is looking out into the distance, and the upper, through which only the sky can be seen behind the cruciform glazing bars, and the mast of a ship that visually connects the upper and

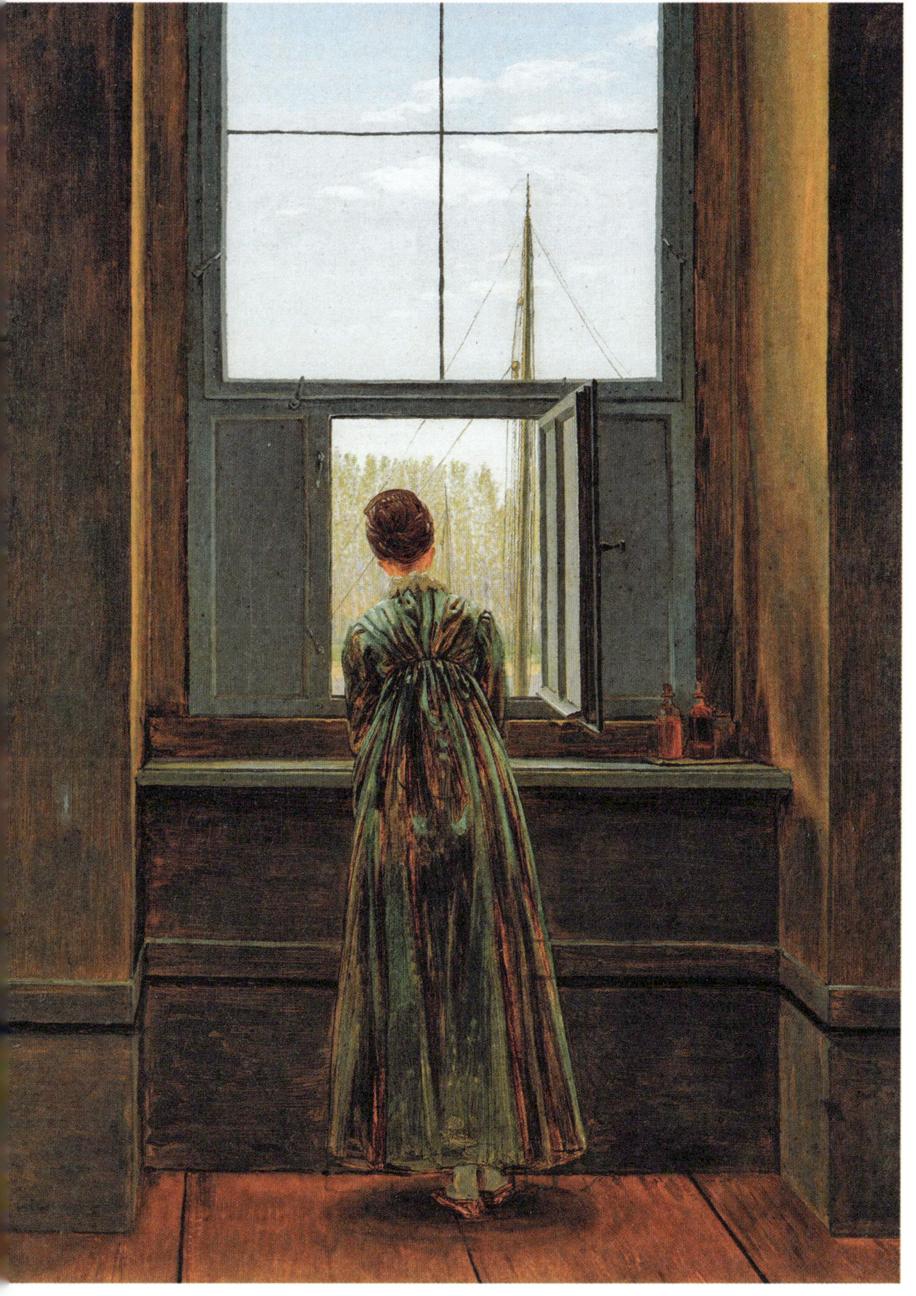

lower windows. The bottom window is framed on all sides, and the view is reduced to the left and right by closed shutters; the top window is cut off by the top edge of the painting, thus evoking the idea of the boundlessness of the sky.

Window representations are paintings within paintings and can be metaphors for painting itself; speaking in favor of this here is the brush and the two glass vessels on the windowsill, which are reminiscent of the work utensils in the studio paintings [→Kersting] of Georg Friedrich Kersting.[→p. 55] The view out of a domestic interior into the outside world is also a motif of longing. It can be interpreted as a longing for the beyond, as a Christian hope—suggested with the window cross—for a life after death.[43] At the same time, the laterally restricted window niche suggests that the worldly room to maneuver of the women figure is finite. She is placed in a position that is marked by the circular shadow of her long dress on the floor. All the more significant seems the gentle inclination with which the woman moves out of the central axis of the painting and turns outward.

Woman at the Window **1822**
Oil on canvas 44 × 37 cm
Alte Nationalgalerie, Staatliche Museen zu Berlin

W → Wanderer

The wanderer is, clearly discernible in German, an *Anderer* (an "other"). "Fremd bin ich eingezogen, fremd zieh ich wieder aus" (I arrived a stranger, a stranger I depart) are the first lines of a Romantic song cycle by Wilhelm Müller (1794–1827). The composer Franz Schubert (1797–1828) set these *Wanderlieder* (wandering songs) to music in 1827 in *Winterreise* (Winter Journey), which one can easily imagine as a soundtrack to Friedrich's painting, as they share central ideas like the longing distant view,→pp. 36–37 the crow →p. 107 as a symbol of death, or the icy cold as a metaphor for a state of mind.→pp. 68–69

Like many of his contemporaries, Friedrich made wandering a foundation of his art. In contrast with the previous generation of artists of Classicism, which was stimulated more by artworks, the Romantics sought their inspiration in nature and visualized their own experiences of nature.

The philosopher F.W.J. Schelling (1775–1854), whose thoughts Friedrich was presumably familiar with through a friend, recommended the following to landscape painters: "Hence, the people in a landscape either must be portrayed as indigenous, as autochthonous, or they must be portrayed as strangers or wanderers recognizable as such by their general disposition, appearance, or even clothing, all of which is alien in relationship to the landscape itself. In this way proximity and distance yet allow themselves to be combined in the landscape in a different sense, and the unique feelings attendant on our conceptions of such juxtaposition can be elicited."[44]

It is revealing against the background of this recommendation to once again consider two figures in Friedrich's landscapes, the *Woman before the Setting* (or: *Rising*) *Sun* (around 1818) →p. 83 and the *Wanderer above the Sea of Fog* (around 1817–18):→p. 59 the one "as autochthonous," ("als gleichsam auf der Stelle gewachsen"), the other "portrayed as strangers or wanderers recognizable as such by their general disposition, appearance, or even clothing."

It is self-explanatory that the wanderer was male in Friedrich's time. "If it were true and my wish were fulfilled," he wrote cheerily to his brother Heinrich in September 1821, "then we would take a lovely journey together," but without the wives, "because that is a trifling matter."[45]

x → Xylography

Friedrich liked to work with pairs of paintings that refer to one another.→p. 45 His drawing *Boy Sleeping/Study of an Axe* from 1802 and the woodcut print based on it entitled *Sleeping Boy on a Grave* are an "inauthentic" pair of images that is nonetheless suited for comparative consideration.

The pen and ink drawing, which is dated January 15, 1802, shows a sleeping boy with his head resting on a tree stump; a bare tree inclines above, a bird, perhaps a raven, perched on a branch. The dead tree is reminiscent of the "Brother of Sleep," death, an association supported by the raven as a bird of misfortune. On February 28, Friedrich added the study of an axe beneath this drawing, which intensifies the latent threatening nature of the scene.

The pen and ink drawing served as the reference for a xylography, which was realized by Friedrich's youngest brother Christian (1779–1843). He was a joiner and a woodcarver, and Friedrich often worked together with him. In this case, the woodcut print is no mere reproduction of the freehand drawing, but instead a kind of comforting reply to the original motif. This is because the boy is here resting on a hill with a grave cross. The linking of sleep and death is loosened in this way; the deceased rests in the grave, hidden from the gaze of the viewer, and is mourned by the figure represented as sleeping. The butterfly over his head can be understood as a symbol for the immortal soul.

Several contemporaries described Friedrich as gloomy and melancholic, and it is said that the early deaths of his mother and of his brother Johann Christoffer → Northwest Passage contributed to his art often revolving around mortality. However, biographical interpretations can impair the view for other aspects. Thus, it should be considered in the case of woodcut prints that these were produced in large numbers and offered at low prices. Perhaps Friedrich hoped to address a broader public through the more pleasing print version with the immortality motif.

Boy Sleeping/Study of an Axe January 15 and February 28, 1802
Pencil, pen, and brown ink 18.1 × 11.6 cm
Kunsthalle Bremen, Kupferstichkabinett

Christian Friedrich after a Drawing by Caspar David Friedrich
Boy Sleeping on a Grave ca. 1802
Woodcut 16.9 × 11.9 cm
Kupferstichkabinett, Staatliche Kunstsammlungen Dresden

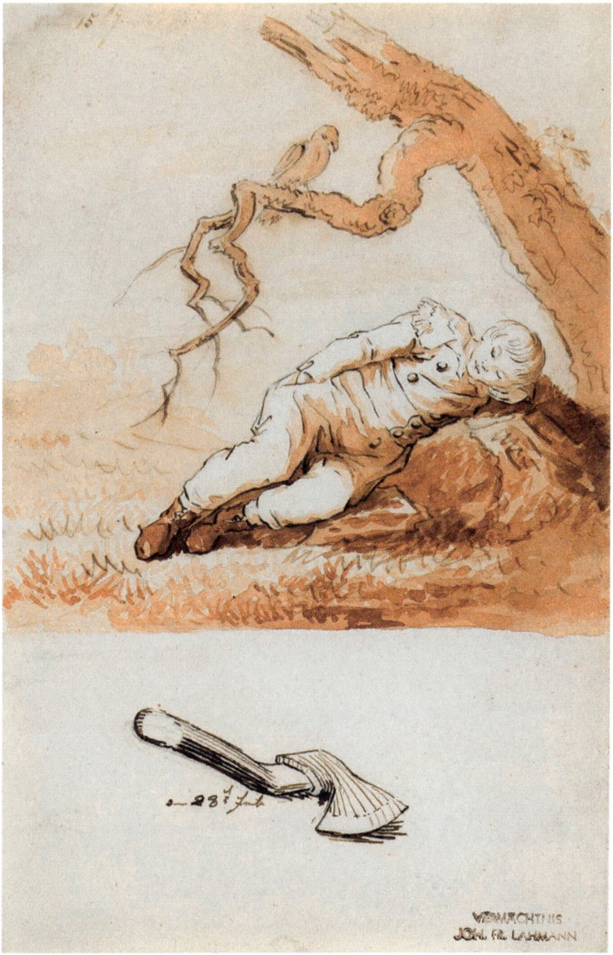

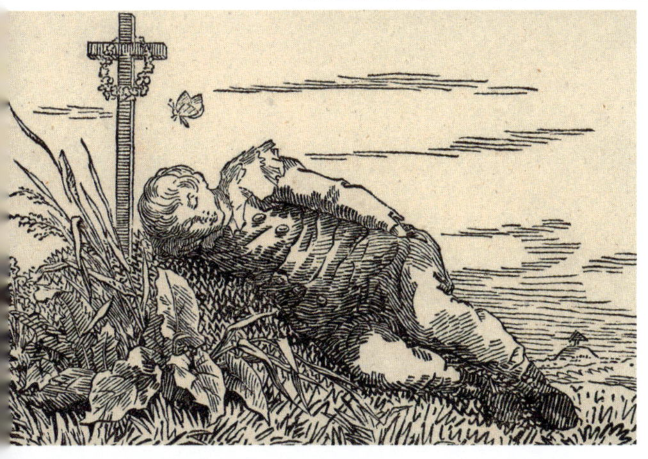

Y→ Young's *Night-Thoughts*

"Nothing could be sadder and more comfortless than this place in the world: the only spark of life in the broad realm of death, the lonesome center point in the lonely circle. The painting, with its two or three mysterious objects, lies there like the apocalypse, as if it had Young's night-thoughts and, because it has nothing other than the frame as a foreground in its uniformity and boundlessness, as if one's eyelids had been cut away."[46]

Heinrich von Kleist's lines about Friedrich's *Monk by the Sea* (around 1808–10) →pp. 110–11 have become almost as famous as the painting itself. They originate from a discussion of Friedrich's extraordinarily reduced composition, which was written by the writers Clemens Brentano and Achim von Arnim and supplemented by Kleist. The text appeared in October 1810 in the *Berliner Abendblätter* and mentions sources that may have inspired Friedrich to his maritime landscape, such as the *Night-Thoughts on Life, Death and Immortality* of the English poet Edward Young (1683–1765) or the seashore sermons of the Rügen pastor and scholar Ludwig Gotthard Kosegarten (1758–1818), who was one of Friedrich's early collectors.

Monk by the Sea was presented at the Berlin Academy exhibition immediately after completion—together with its same-sized counterpart *Abbey in the Oakwood* (around 1809–10), where King Frederick William III purchased the

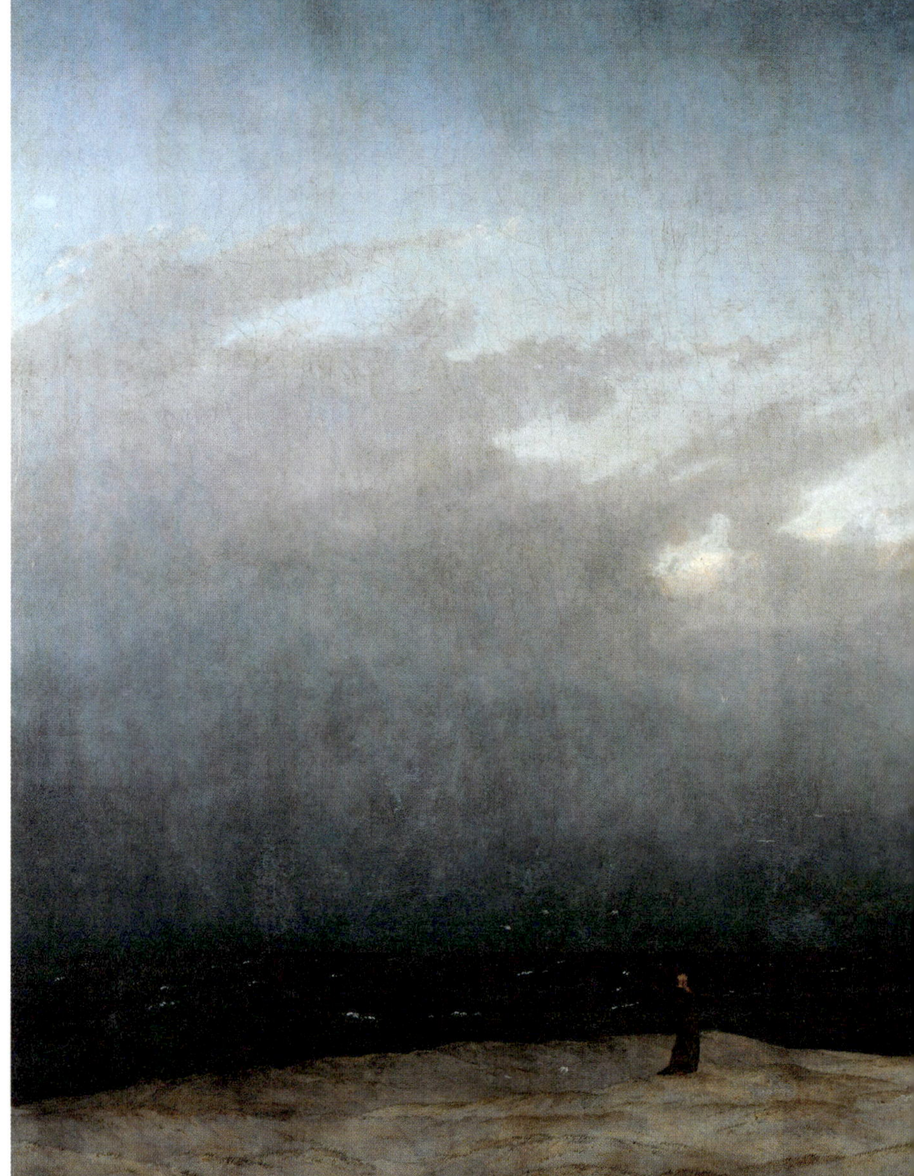

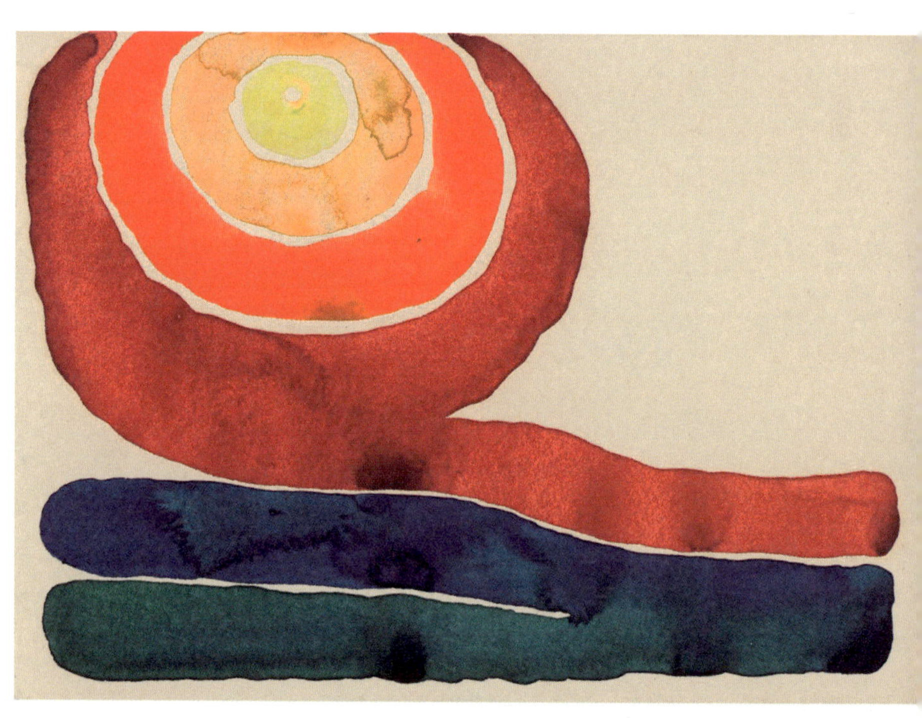

pair of paintings at the request of the fifteen-year-old Prussian Crown Prince. This was a considerable success for the artist, after his *Tetschen Altar* had resulted in such a public controversy the year before.→ Jeers

With *Monk by the Sea*, Friedrich, as Kleist recognized, had "without a doubt broken completely new ground in the field of his art," which would lead far into the twentieth century. The American art historian Robert Rosenblum thus drew a line of tradition in the mid-1970s that extends from Friedrich's "somber, luminous void" to the formally reduced abstractions of American painters like Barnett Newman and Mark Rothko and to the archetypical landscape motifs of Georgia O'Keeffe.[47]

Monk by the Sea ca. 1808–1810
Oil on canvas 110 × 171.5 cm
Alte Nationalgalerie, Staatliche Museen zu Berlin

Georgia O'Keeffe
Evening Star No. III 1917
Watercolor on paper 22.7 × 30.4 cm
Museum of Modern Art, New York

z → Zittau Mountains

One must imagine Friedrich as a political person.→Politics He explained in a letter to Ernst Moritz Arndt (1769–1860) from March 12, 1814: "It does not surprise me whatsoever that no monuments have been erected, neither those that signify the great cause of the people, nor the magnanimous deeds of individual German men. And nothing great of this kind will happen as long as we remain the servants of princes. Where the people have no voice, the people will also not be allowed to feel and honor itself."[48]

Friedrich had in fact already designed a monument for the fighters of the Wars of Liberation against the Napoleonic occupation, which he had also experienced in Dresden. With his painting *Hutten's Tomb* (around 1823–24), he once again refers to this unrealized project. The concrete occasion was the tercentenary of the death of Ulrich von Hutten (1488–1523), who was persecuted for his criticism of the secularized papacy and as a champion of the Lutheran Reformation. In Friedrich's time, one also saw a role model for the freedom fighters against Napoleon and for German patriots in the Renaissance humanist, who wanted to throw off the "Roman yoke."

Friedrich transports Hutten's tomb, which is actually found on an island in Lake Zurich, to a fictitious backdrop. He had already found the template for the Gothic ruin that provides the backdrop of the painting in 1810 on the Oybin, a massif in the Zittau Mountains. From a present-day perspective, this pictorial element seems astonishingly contradictory, as the Gothic cathedral is an invention from Catholic France, and the monastery on the Oybin was dissolved at the beginning of the sixteenth century in the course of the Reformation, to which Friedrich felt a religious affiliation, and was left to decay as a result.

At Hutten's tomb, a figure in old German costume looks at the names and dates inscribed into the sarcophagus: "Jahn 1813," "Arndt 1813," "Stein 1813," "Görres 1821," and "F. Scharnhorst." Figures like Arndt or the so-called *Turnvater* (roughly "Father of Gymnastics") Friedrich Ludwig Jahn (1778–1852) are today the subject of controversies due to anti-Semitic, nationalist, militaristic, and Francophobe statements. Exemplary of this is the decision of the University of Greifswald →Greifswald from 2017 to shed its name of "Ernst-Moritz-Arndt-Universität," assigned to it in 1933. *Hutten's Tomb* is thus not only a commemorative picture of the Wars of Liberation and national liberal, republican ideals. It can also serve as a springboard into European (art) history and raise the question of how meanings can be generated, shifted, and decoded.

Hutten's Tomb **ca. 1823/24**
Oil on canvas 93.5 × 73.4 cm
Klassik Stiftung Weimar

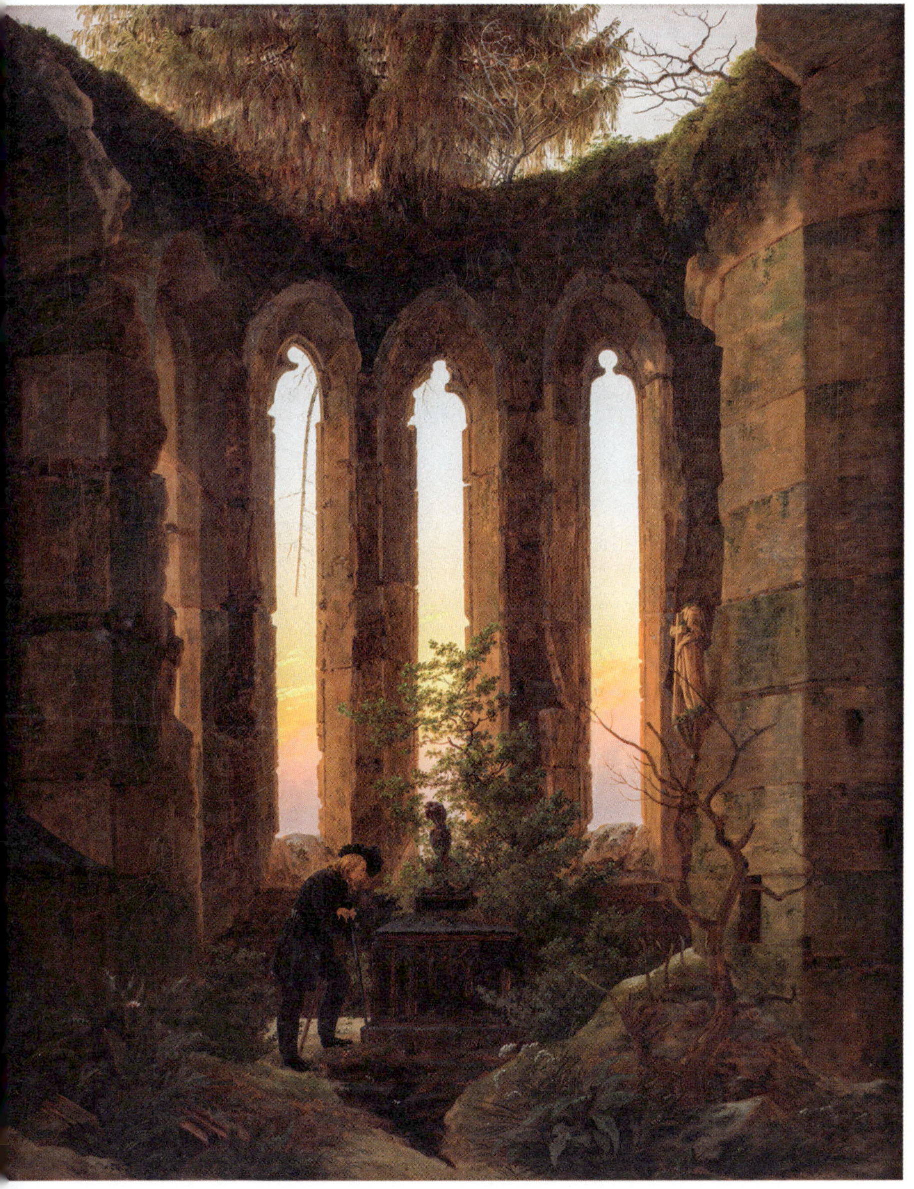

1 Letter to Grand Duchess Alexandra Feodorovna, June 23, 1821, cited from *Caspar David Friedrich in Briefen und Bekenntnissen*, ed. Sigrid Hinz (East Berlin: Henschelverlag, 1968), p. 236.
2 See the entry "Baum in der Landschaft," in *Caspar David Friedrich 1774–1840*, ed. Werner Hofmann, exh. cat. Hamburger Kunsthalle (Munich: Prestel, 1974), pp. 46–47.
3 Johannes Grave leaves the question of the time of day open; see Grave, *Caspar David Friedrich* (Munich: Prestel, 2022; 1st ed. 2012), fig. 176, p. 205.
4 So is the thesis of Detlef Stapf, "Caspar David Friedrich – Eine Biographie," in *Caspar David Friedrich und die Vorboten der Romantik*, ed. Wolf Eiermann and David Schmidhauser, exh. cat. Museum Georg Schäfer Schweinfurt; Kunst Museum Winterthur/Reinhart am Stadtgarten (Munich: Hirmer Verlag, 2023), pp. 27–35, here p. 33. On the critique of Stapf, see Birte Frenssen et al., "Problematische Thesen von Detlef Stapf zu Caspar David Friedrich," https://archiv.ub.uni-heidelberg.de/artdok/8571/.
5 Jens Christian Jensen, *Caspar David Friedrich: Leben und Werk* (Cologne: Dumont, 1974), p. 134.
6 Grave, *Caspar David Friedrich*, pp. 134–35.
7 *Caspar David Friedrich in Briefen und Bekenntnissen*, ed. Hinz, p. 21.
8 Karl-Ludwig Hoch, *Caspar David Friedrich: Unbekannte Dokumente seines Lebens* (Dresden: Verlag der Kunst, 1985), pp. 62–63.
9 Grave, *Caspar David Friedrich*, p. 65.
10 Ibid., p. 135.
11 Cited from Joseph Leo Koerner, *Caspar David Friedrich and the Subject of Landscape* (London: Reaktion Books, 1990), p. 64.
12 Cited from ibid, p. 66.
13 See Koerner, *Caspar David Friedrich and the Subject of the Landscape*, pp. 91–93.
14 Cited from Werner Hofmann, *Caspar David Friedrich: Naturwirklichkeit und Kunstwahrheit* (Munich: C.H. Beck, 2000), p. 33.
15 See *Caspar David Friedrich 1774–1840*, ed. Hofmann, no. 139, pp. 224–25; Grave, *Caspar David Friedrich*, p. 216.
16 See Grave, *Caspar David Friedrich*, p. 114.
17 Cited from Hofmann, *Caspar David Friedrich*, p. 177.
18 The letter is printed in Hofmann, *Caspar David Friedrich*, pp. 264–65.
19 On this in detail, see Joseph Leo Koerner, *Caspar David Friedrich and the Subject of Landscape*, pp. 47–63.
20 Printed again in Hofmann, *Caspar David Friedrich*, pp. 275–80.
21 Cited from Hofmann, *Caspar David Friedrich*, p. 280.
22 Cited from Hofmann, *Caspar David Friedrich*, p. 282.
23 Jensen, *Caspar David Friedrich*, p. 24.
24 "Voilá un homme, qui a découvert la tragédie du paysage!" Cited from Grave, *Caspar David Friedrich*, p. 21.
25 Cited from James Knowlson, *Damned to Fame: The Life of Samuel Beckett* (New York: Grove Press, 1996), p. 254.
26 Thus, the reading of Peter Märker; see Grave, *Caspar David Friedrich*, p. 206.
27 Knowlson, *Damned to Fame*, p. 254.
28 All quotes from Jensen, *Caspar David Friedrich: Leben und Werk*, pp. 203–04.
29 Grave, *Caspar David Friedrich*, p. 25.
30 Cited from *Caspar David Friedrich in Briefen und Bekenntnissen*, ed. Hinz, p. 218.
31 Cited from Frank Richter, *Carl Gustav Carus: Der Malerfreund Caspar David Friedrichs und seine Landschaften* (Dresden: Verlag der Kunst, 2009), p. 24.
32 The terms originate from the art historian Kurt Karl Eberlein, cited from Werner Hofmann, "Vorwort des Herausgebers," in *Caspar David Friedrich und die deutsche Nachwelt*, ed. Werner Hofmann (Frankfurt: Suhrkamp, 1974), pp. 7–14, here p. 9. Hofmann uses the word *Weiheaura* on p. 13.
33 Cited from Koerner, *Caspar David Friedrich and the Subject of Landscape*, p. 76.
34 Detlef Stapf, *Caspar David Friedrich: Die Biografie* (Berlin: Okapi, 2019), p. 43.
35 Cited from Hofmann, *Caspar David Friedrich*, p. 285.
36 Jensen, *Caspar David Friedrich: Leben und Werk*, p. 77.
37 See Grave, *Caspar David Friedrich*, pp. 74–83.

38 See Werner Busch, *Caspar David Friedrich* (Munich: C.H. Beck, 2021), pp. 31–32.
39 On this, see Koerner, *Caspar David Friedrich and the Subject of Landscape,* p. 192.
40 Cited from *Caspar David Friedrich in Briefen und Bekenntnissen*, ed. Hinz, pp. 70–73, here p. 73.
41 On this in more detail, see Busch, *Caspar David Friedrich*, pp. 62–79.
42 See ibid., p. 38–42.
43 Helmut Börsch-Supan, *Caspar David Friedrich* (Munich: Prestel, 1973), p. 128.
44 Cited from Koerner, *Caspar David Friedrich and the Subject of the Landscape*, p. 218.
45 Cited from *Caspar David Friedrich in Briefen und Bekenntnissen*, ed. Hinz, p. 48.
46 Heinrich von Kleist, Clemens Brentano, and Achim von Arnim, "Verschiedene Empfindungen vor einer Seelandschaft von Friedrich, worauf ein Kapuziner," *Berliner Abendblätter*, October 13, 1810, reprinted in Hofmann, *Caspar David Friedrich: Naturwirklichkeit und Kunstwahrheit*, pp. 282–85, here p. 282.
47 Robert Rosenblum, *Modern Painting and the Northern Romantic Tradition: Friedrich to Rothko* (New York: Harper and Row, 1975), p. 10.
48 Cited from Hofmann, *Caspar David Friedrich*, p. 264.

Biography

September 5, 1774 Caspar David Friedrich is born in Greifswald, then part of Swedish Pomerania.

ca. 1789/90 Instruction from the university drawing teacher Johann Gottfried Quistorp.

1794–1798 Friedrich studies at the Academy of Fine Arts in Copenhagen.

1798 Relocation to Dresden and enrollment at the art academy there.

1801/02 Extended visit back home; stays in Greifswald, Neubrandenburg, and on the island of Rügen.

1805 Participation in the Weimar prize competition; Friedrich receives half of the first prize for two sepia drawings.

1806 Another stay in Neubrandenburg, Greifswald and on Rügen.

1807 Journey to Northern Bohemia.

1808 Friedrich exhibits the *Tetschen Altar* in his studio.

1810 Tour through the Giant Mountains with Georg Friedrich Kersting. Johann Wolfgang von Goethe visits Friedrich in his studio. *Monk by the Sea* and *Abbey in the Oakwood* are exhibited at the Berlin academy and purchased by the Prussian king. Friedrich is elected a member of the Berlin academy.

1811 Hike through the Harz.

1813 Dresden is occupied by French troops, Friedrich flees to Krippen in the Elbe Sandstone Mountains.

1816 Friedrich is accepted as a member of the Dresden Academy of Fine Arts.

1818 Marriage with Caroline Bommer; trips to Greifswald, Stralsund, and Rügen.

1819 Birth of Friedrich's first daughter.

1820 Acquaintance with the Russian poet and state councilor Vasily Andreyevich Zhukovsky, who arranged for numerous paintings by Friedrich to be added to collections in Moscow and St. Petersburg.

1823 Birth of Friedrich's second daughter.

1824 Friedrich is appointed professor by the Dresden academy, but does not receive the desired post as head of the landscape class. Illness. Birth of Friedrich's first son.

1835 Friedrich suffers a stroke.

May 7, 1840 Friedrich dies in Dresden.

Photo Credits

Frontispiece: bpk / Kupferstichkabinett, SMB / Jörg P. Anders
pp. 8/9: Alte Nationalgalerie, Staatliche Museen zu Berlin / Jörg P. Anders (CC BY-NC-SA)
p. 10: *Caspar David Friedrich. Die Briefe*, 2nd edition, ed. Hermann Zschoche (Hamburg: ConferencePoint Verlag, 2006), p. 9
pp. 13, 16, 36/37, 49, 55, 63, 68/69, 72 top, 83, 117: The publisher's and author's archives
pp. 20/21, 28/29, 40, 45, 59, 91 bottom, 99, 107 bottom, 110/111: Wikimedia Commons
p. 25: bpk / Hamburger Kunsthalle / Elke Walford
pp. 32/33: photo: Belvedere, Vienna
p. 42: Stiftung Preußische Schlösser und Gärten Berlin-Brandenburg / Pfauder, Wolfgang (2011) (CC BY-NC-SA)
p. 60: Letzte Generation
p. 72 bottom: Private collection, courtesy of Talabardon & Gautier, Paris / Art Digital Studio
p. 79: photo: © Rheinisches Bildarchiv Köln, rba_c004682
p. 86: © Albertina, Vienna
p. 91 top: bpk / Hessen Kassel Heritage
p. 95: Pommersches Landesmuseum Greifswald, Digitale Bibliothek Mecklenburg-Vorpommern
p. 107 top: Kunsthalle Bremen – Der Kunstverein in Bremen (CC BY-NC-SA)
p. 112: © Georgia O'Keeffe Museum / VG Bild-Kunst, Bonn 2023

Colophon

The concept of the A-Z series is based on an idea by Ulf Küster.

Author Barbara Hess
Copyediting Aaron Bogart
Translations Kenneth Friend
Project management Fabian Reichel
Graphic design Torsten Köchlin, Joana Katte
Typeface Scto Grotesk A
Production Thomas Lemaître
Reproductions DLG Graphic, Paris
Paper Munken Lynx, 150 g/m^2
Printing DZS GRAFIK, d. o. o., Ljubljana

Published by
Hatje Cantz Verlag GmbH
Mommsenstrasse 27
10629 Berlin
Germany
www.hatjecantz.com

A Ganske Publishing Group Company

ISBN 978-3-7757-5567-2
(English edition)

ISBN 978-3-7757-5566-5
(German edition)

Printed in Slovenia

Cover illustration
Detail from Caspar David Friedrich
Woman in Front of the Setting
(or: *Rising*) *Sun*
ca. 1818 (see p. 83)

Frontispiece
Detail from Caspar David Friedrich
Self-Portrait ca. 1810
Black chalk on paper 22.8 × 18.2 cm
Kupferstichkabinett,
Staatliche Museen zu Berlin